Elkheart

The Nearby Faraway: A Personal Journey through the Heart of the West

A Hunter's Heart: Honest Essays on Blood Sport (editor)

Ghost Grizzlies: Does the Great Bear Still Haunt Colorado?

Confessions of a Barbarian: Selections from the Journals of Edward Abbey (editor)

Earth Apples: The Poetry of Edward Abbey (editor)

Racks: The Natural History of Antlers and the Animals That Wear Them

Among the Aspen

Big Sky, Fair Land: The Environmental Essays of A. B. Guthrie, Jr. (editor)

Among the Elk

Elkheart

A Personal Tribute to Wapiti and Their World

David Petersen

Foreword by Dan Crockett

Johnson Books

BOULDER

Published in the United States by Johnson Books, a division of Johnson Publishing Company, 1880 South 57th Court, Boulder, Colorado 80301. E-mail: books@jpcolorado.com

9 8 7 6 5 4 3 2

Cover design: Debra B. Topping
Cover illustration: *Nightfall in September* (detail), lithograph by Russell Chatham

Library of Congress Cataloging-in-Publication Data
Petersen, David, 1946–
  Elkheart: a personal tribute to wapiti and their world / David Petersen: foreword by Dan Crockett.
      p.   cm.
  Includes bibliographical references.
  ISBN 1-55566-224-2 (cloth: alk. paper). — ISBN 1-55566-225-0 (pbk.: alk. paper)
  1. Elk—San Juan Mountains (Colo. and N.M.)   2. Zoology—San Juan Mountains (Colo. and N.M.)   I. Title.
QL737.U55P474   1998
599.65 ' 42 ' 097883—dc21   98-25871
                                                                CIP

Printed in the United States by
Johnson Printing
1880 South 57th Court
Boulder, Colorado 80301

for Erica Fresquez and Jamin Grigg —
Elkhearts and good hearts, both

Contents

Acknowledgments

WITHOUT THE INSPIRATION, indulgence, understanding and independence granted me across the past two decades by my live-in editor, companion and keeper, not only would these stories never have been written, neither would I have known the exuberantly joyful, somewhat eccentric life they loosely chronicle. Artist, singer, wood nymph, wife: I love you, Caroline.

Special thanks go also to my good friends at the Rocky Mountain Elk Foundation of Missoula, Montana. It was RMEF communications director Lance Schelvan who, once upon a happy time, invited me to become a *Bugle* contributor, thus pointing me down the wapiti-worn path leading to this humble homage. Dan Crockett, who recklessly volunteered to write a foreword to this Politically Incorrect and turbulent tome, as *Bugle* editor, provided first publication (in slightly different form) for many of the essays I've herded together here under the esoteric title *Elkheart*. David Stalling, *Bugle* conservation editor and fellow recovering Marine (I flew the perfectly good helicopters that Dave so loved to leap from), has been a deep well of information and aid throughout the months-long process of fitting together this puzzle (pizzle?) of pages, especially regarding the nightmarish topic of elk ranching. (I'm not kidding; both us Daves have suffered nightmares while researching and writing about the very scary topic of privatization and commercialization of wildlife.)

Canada's most honorable Dr. Valerius Geist has long been an inspiration, not only as a world-class field biologist, but as a courageously outspoken wildlife issues ethicist—right up there with Colorado's Tom "Bear Man" Beck and eco-journalist Ted Williams, each of whom has suffered, and survived, personal and professional attacks simply for telling the truth. I thank you all for helping to stiffen my own resolve by sterling example, and especially for wading through, candidly commenting on and wisely calming (somewhat) my rant against elk ranching herein to follow.

East across the Continental Divide from here, up in bustling Boulder town, my ever-patient editor Stephen Topping, the ever-clever Mira Perrizo (who, like me, is carried off to Oz by the boisterous bugling of braggish bull elk on enchanted autumn eves) and every last one of the other fine folk at Johnson Books, have been an unmitigated pleasure to work with: past, present and (it is mine to hope) future.

Once again, I am honored to have the ethereal art of Russell Chatham gracing the cover of a book of mine. Thank you Russ and Carol. Likewise, I am grateful for the artful cover design of Debra Topping.

I wish you one and all the wild heady blessing of elk scent on your boots.

Foreword

Hunting Hope

IN 1983, DAVID PETERSEN landed assignments from *Mother Earth News* and *Writer's Digest* to interview a man whose words had done much to shape the way Petersen ordered his life. So when he first sat down with Edward Abbey, he could have easily indulged in a little awestruck fawning. Instead, he began peppering Abbey with tough questions. Abbey must have appreciated Petersen's free-spirited sinew, for the two of them talked and drank beer all through the afternoon and deep into the night. Somewhere in the midst of this rambling conversation, Petersen asked, "Are you an atheist?"

"I am an *earthiest*," Abbey rumbled. "I stand for what I stand on."

This remark chimed through Petersen like a bull's bugle bringing light and heat long before the sun first colors the serrated peaks. He later wrote:

Earthiesm, as I've come to understand and embrace it, is nothing more or less than contemporary animism. And an animist, of course, is nothing less than a heathen, that primitive, savage, uncivilized, beastly human form described by Ambrose Bierce as "a benighted creature who has the folly to worship something that he can see and feel."

Bingo!

Guilty as charged, Petersen does indeed worship all of the natural world his senses can absorb. He celebrates the cidery tang of mist on fallen aspen leaves; the hail-on-the-roof percussion of whitetail bucks in combat; fingers of wind rumpling the guard hairs on a sow grizzly's hump in the same way they once stroked a thousand miles of head-high grass; the good hard weight of an elk quarter. In previous books, Petersen has paid tribute to aspens, antlers and grizzly bears. Each of these, bears especially, figure prominently once more in this collection of essays. In fact, though reluctant to speak in what he calls "dreamy terms," Petersen suggests that bears are his spiritual totems.

Yet his wife of eighteen years did not dub him Bearheart. No, Caroline's affectionate, half-serious nickname for him is Elkheart. For Petersen, bears are sacred; not to be hunted. And perhaps there are aspects of our relationship with a wild animal that can only be had by hunting it.

This is the kind of mushy pronouncement bound to arouse indignation in anyone who loves deer but finds the idea of killing one unthinkable. Does the man who crawls his truck up and down logging roads while scanning for a buck to shoot (preferably on the uphill side of the rig) have a more profound connection with this animal than the poet who sees in its eye an infinite well of tenderness, or the biologist who has spent enough time among the herd to identify individual animals at a glance and delight in their idiosyncrasies? Hell no. But I believe that people for whom honorable conduct is an indelible part of the hunt can, in fact, know their quarry in a way which others cannot.

Even this must seem maddening to those who do not hunt. How can killers claim the high ground?

I could say, because hunters are the only ones who accept the truth. I could argue that those who hunt not only acknowledge but accept personal responsibility for the reality that we all kill, that every creature exists at a cost to other creatures, that life is built on death. But I know far too many caring people who grasp these truths at every level of their being—people who try to lead their lives in such a way as to cause the least harm and the most good—yet are simply unwilling, perhaps genuinely unable, to take the deer's life.

Choosing to hunt raises no one to higher ground. It merely opens a pathway into a different land. This is a magical place where insights into the spirits of both the hunted and the hunter may be revealed. It is a land forever tinged with sorrow.

Petersen knows this country intimately. For nearly forty years, he has seized and savored every opportunity to hunt whitetails, wild turkeys, antelope, mule deer, caribou, Coues deer, geese, grouse, quail, snowshoe hares. His drive to come to know each of these creatures and to hunt them honorably and well is pure and fierce. But let me be clear. Petersen is an elk bum.

Sure, he's a writer. A damned good one. But he doesn't do novels or screenplays or ad copy. On top of that, he insists on telling the truth and speaking with passion about the things he believes. He turns down assignments that compromise his hammer-forged sense of integrity. No matter what the potential rewards, he shuns publishers who put profits before principles. He dismisses the idea of accepting freebies—cutting-edge gear, private ranch hunts—in exchange for the fatuous, banal endorsements that masquerade as articles in too many outdoor magazines. As a result, his income oscillates around that arbitrary level our government calls the poverty line. Yet he enjoys one of the highest standards of living of anyone I know.

It's awfully easy to romanticize someone else's life. But in exchange for his meager earnings, Petersen writes almost exclusively what he wants to write. With allowances for occasional immersions in deserts, canyons and other mountains, he goes out walking in the San Juan Mountains for some part of nearly every day. More than three hundred days a year, he's out there, following the ravens to a cow elk whose fat melted away before the snow did, searching for shed antlers among patchy snowdrifts, grinning at the first wobbly steps of a calf, watching great bulbous antlers grow at a rate more commonly associated with tropical vines. Then for thirty days he *hunts*.

Because he uses a bow, Colorado allows him to pursue elk for the entire month of September. And that's what he does. At least as much of choice as necessity, he seldom roams anything but public land. His conscience is always his only guide; usually his only companion. During the eight years I've known him, Petersen has never missed more than a handful of days out of any hunting season. His wife Caroline can attest that each September day spent without bow in hand is heralded by grudging laments verging on ululations.

"He's changed over the years," she jokes. "These days, he doesn't want to *kill* an elk nearly so much as he wants to *be* an elk."

Could be. But I believe him when he says, "More and more, what I want most is the hunt itself."

Don't get the wrong idea. While Petersen makes a compelling argument that hunters can and should be the greatest champions of the wild, there's scarcely a hunting tale in this book. Most of it is pure natural history; observations and reflections about elk and other wild things. Petersen is a lover of natural mystery. And his boundless curiosity has a pleasantly eclectic bent, ranging from the small and funky to the enormous and unknowable. Do elk really need salt licks, he wonders, or are licks just the cervid equivalent of our superfluous salt shakers? Could there be a symbiotic relationship between aspens and elk? How and why have antlers evolved, and what might they eventually look like?

The questions he seems to enjoy most, though, are: "What do animals actually feel and know?" and "How do they share their feelings and knowledge with one another?" This is the sort of inquiry that sends most hunters and biologists crawdadding back to the safe view that animals function purely on instinct.

Old-school wildlife biologists detest anthropomorphism — assigning human characteristics, emotions in particular, to animals — but as a mere humble hunter, woodsman and watcher, I am free to believe my own senses, Petersen writes. It is our fortune that his senses are attuned to the nuances that make wandering the woods not only an act of endless fascination, but a form of communion. There is a specific irony in how far our society has wandered from hunting cultures around the world which for thousands of years reverenced the power and knowledge of animals. I am reminded of that moment in Richard Nelson's wonderful study of the Koyukon people and their relationships with the natural and supernatural worlds, *Make Prayers to the Raven,* when a tribal elder tells him, "Every animal knows way more than you do."

It is particularly refreshing to see a frequent contributor to hunting magazines goring the comfortable notion that other animals are somehow of lesser importance than humans. In these times, of course, anyone fascinated by the mysteries of wild animals and wild places carries a burden of fear, despair and rage over the way humans are behaving toward everything else on this planet. As Petersen says, *We all need wildness in our lives, whether we realize it or not. For if we allow wild nature to die, murdered by human greed and stupidity, our humanity will die with it.*

You don't have to be an animist to feel this way. No matter who or what you worship, if you love the wild, you have tasted the bitter bile that comes from seeing the things you cherish brutalized. Let me assure you, Petersen has tasted it often. When he struggles to cleanse his soul, he is capable of thunderous ranting.

But his anger never springs from hatred or mean-spiritedness. On the contrary, it arises from his sense of responsibility to the things he loves—elk, mountains, the hunt, freedom. You can hear that love ringing through when he implores, *Being good neighbors to elk and other wildlife, and to the dwindling and tortured habitat they depend on for their very survival, especially in winter, isn't all that big a deal, isn't so much to ask of the proud citizens of America the Beautiful. Is it?*

In September 1989, I started helping edit *Bugle,* the Rocky Mountain Elk Foundation's magazine. Because this brash young magazine was offering fresh, critical thinking on habitat conservation, elk ecology and hunting, David Petersen had found it long before I did. When I was first handed one of Petersen's stories to edit, I felt like a batboy being asked to help Tony Gwynn hone his chops. Clearly, he knew a hell of a lot more than I did about elk and hunting and writing. As it turned out, he never let this knowledge get in the way of making a good thing better.

After you edit someone's work for a while—working together as if you were building a mortarless stone wall, trading turns fitting in the next rock—you start to feel like you know them, even though you haven't met. But you're never quite sure. When Dave and Caroline made plans in 1990 to stop by our cabin on their way to Glacier, I felt a little trepidation. What if he brought along a photo album the size of a Denver phone book to highlight his last few hunting seasons? What if he turned out to be one of those shrill enviro-bores with a penchant for grave and gloomy monologues? I needn't have worried. Dave's warm, down-to-earth grace immediately convinced me that I did indeed know him, and that I wanted to know him better.

Three springs ago, my wife and I and our then-two-year-old daughter spent a few days in early June camping and hiking and watching with Dave and Caroline. We were in a sweeping valley in Yellowstone National Park. In the spring there, it is almost possible to feel life hurtling out of the earth. You can sit on a hill and find yourself nearly dizzied. It's like watching the wild, random grace of the Perseids, except that each showering meteor, each shooting star is a bison, sandhill crane, mountain harebell, northern leopard frog, antelope, curlew, badger, pale swallowtail, grizzly bear, elk. Especially elk. Go to a hilltop at dawn. Turn in a slow circle. You will see elk at every point of your orbit; in the foreground, at the outermost edges, shimmering on the periphery. More elk come here to give birth than perhaps any other place on Earth.

When this valley fills with elk calves, it sounds the same clarion call for Yellowstone's grizzlies as an Alaskan river swelling with salmon. The big bears come hunting. Coyotes and jittery black bears join them. And that spring, a hunter so long absent from this place as to seem only a ghost was there once more, too.

One evening in a cottonwood grove beside the river that defines this valley we grilled a pair of mallards I had shot on the winter solstice. Even as the ducks sizzled, we could see the pearl-gray forms of two wolves lolling perhaps a quarter mile away across the river. Dave's eyes shone like the tarns that everywhere returned the gift of sky.

"For once we did the right thing," he exulted. "We had to do it the arrogant way, with darts and ear tags and pens. But they're back. They're back!"

He raised his glass in the direction of the wolves and added quietly, "Happy hunting."

That's how it is with this book. There is wisdom, anger, joy, sorrow. There is clear-eyed acknowledgment of our loss of wildness, of what we are doing to the Earth. But always you can find hope murmuring through these essays like meltwater invisible beneath fractured granite.

Happy hunting.

Dan Crockett
Missoula, Montana

Forewarning

Disclamations from the Outhouse

BEWARE: THIS IS NO authoritative treatise on elk, nor on much of anything else, as I am no authority on much of anything. In fact, I've spent most of my wayward life rebelling against authority—no, let's make that "authoritarianism"—the stain of which iconoclasm doubtless yellows these pages.

Sniffing on down this same confessional trail, I'm tempted to paraphrase grizzly champion Doug Peacock, who has declared, "I'm glad I'm not a scientist; scientists have to prove things, and I only want to learn." Quite so. But then, we can hope that *good* scientists will learn a few things along the road to working out their proofs; and frankly, if I had it all to do again, I likely would become a field biologist—assuming I could conquer all those deadly boring college courses (math, chemistry, statistics) that defeated me the first go-round, relegating me to this lowly life of literary longing ... and assuming further that I could suffer the insufferable government bureaucracies most biologists must endure, and which take idealistic young people and whip them down to desk-riding size. Come to think of it, Peacock has a point.

If you're seriously interested in the scientific subtleties of our deer friend *Cervus elaphus*—as interested as I have been these past twenty years—I defer and refer you to *Elk of North Amer-*

ica: Ecology and Management, a massive tome that's literally obese with scholarly (elk) meat.

For a far more concise, cogent, personable and (I must say) enjoyable summary of the wapiti essentials—all that most of us will ever need or care to know—I enthusiastically recommend *Elk Country*, by the good Canadian Dr. Valerius Geist, among the world's leading wapiti scholars and a whole lot more. (For full citations on these and other works alluded to here and henceforth, feel free to consult the bibliography I've labored so dutifully, if not diligently, to provide.)

While admittedly there's a sprinkling of wapiti biology in what follows—begged, borrowed and filched from Val Geist and many another bona fide biologist—*Elkheart* is not nearly so much about science as it is about, well ... love. Love for and from the steep rocky heart of elk country, where I live the year 'round, and around, sponging up the summer's sun and enduring winter's snow. It's a love having grown from close daily fellowship with raw-boned nature and attentive, at times perhaps even semi-thoughtful, observation of elk and their wild woolly comrades—the bears and bugs and others—their habits and their habitats. That's it.

Well, that's it for the most part. Additionally, unavoidably I suppose, these essays, stories, polemics and musings are also about me. For such selfish self-indulgence I can and do apologize, but will never recant.

In *Scenery and the Sense of Sight*, art scholar Vaughn Cornish, in discussing "sources of pleasure in the visual aspect," notes that "when no association of ideas can be found to account for the ecstatic mood [so often evoked by viewing good art], it is often attributed to some spiritual quality higher than ordinary thought." It's just such an "aesthetic ecstasy" I experience at the best of magical moments out amongst the elk and the bears, beneath the shivering aspens. This is what I know, and this—not science, not art, but the overwhelming ecstasy to be found only through personal immersion in truly wild nature—this is what I have labored, through this artless assemblage of scribblings, to evoke, to relay, to trigger in universal memory and imagination.

Big pond, little fish.

If I see myself as anything but a lover of wildness and freedom and the wilderness that embodies and enables both, it is, I suppose, as an old-style naturalist—which, by my lights, is anyone who loves the natural world sufficiently to make it a focus of his or her life—not a life's work, necessarily, but a persevering personal passion.

Passion enough, per example, to get up and out long before light and stay out deep after dark, day after month after year—walking, crawling when necessary, uncounted miles in all manner of weather, on the trail of ... what?

On the trail of mystery, that's what. In pursuit of natural-borne truths. Seeking to revive the joyful bond with nature inculcated in our very (human) being through millions of years of symbiotic, synergistic evolution alongside—eating and being eaten by—large wild animals ... an instinctive joy that ten millennia of pastoral-agricultural-industrial-urban drudgery have coated with a sludge of cultural crap, but which stubbornly refuses to die.

Perhaps you know another such a one as me. This book is for that one.

—*from the Outhouse*
San Juan Mountains, Colorado

His voice came from the hills somewhere, sharp-pitched and sorrowful, and threaded through the night like a needle.
—A. B. Guthrie, Jr., from *The Big Sky*

Hippity-hoppity ... here comes the wapiti!
—Anon

Among the Elk at Play

Has joy any survival value in the operation of evolution? I
suspect that it does; I suspect that the morose and fearful are
doomed to quick extinction. Where there is no joy there can be
no courage; and without courage all other virtues are useless.
                                                              —Edward Abbey

MY YEAR-ROUND HOME, the pine-board epitome of "be it ever
so humble," is a tiny self-built cabin squatting at eight thousand
feet in the San Juan Mountains of southwest Colorado. Although
pug-ugly growth and subdividing across the past few years have
taken their toll, it's still a nice place to live, with distinct annual
seasons. And every autumn, it's an elkheart's paradise.

Typically for that time of year, this time of year, autumn after
golden autumn, I dress for work—moccasins, sweat pants, t-shirt—
kiss Caroline so-long and make the morning commute—about
thirty feet—to the storage shed cum office I call the Outhouse
(seems appropriate, given what's produced within), there (here) to
ply my dubious trade until mid-afternoon. I then commute back
home, eat a late lunch, shower, pull on camouflage—like morph-
ing into a second skin, with a whole new (actually, infinitely old)
worldview built in—hang a pack on my back and chug cheerfully
up a nearby mountain for an evening's play.

Last year was a drought year and by hanging out near spring
pools I saw elk almost every day. In this semi-arid country, water

is a wildlife magnet. But this summer has been exceptionally wet, and across three evenings spent so far watching springs, I've seen not only no elk, but no fresh tracks nor even a pile of summer-soft droppings. It's as if the rains have washed the wapiti away; at the least, the animals are certainly not thirsty. Nor so far have I heard any bugling, but that's typical for so early in the rut.

🦌

Today is Sunday, thank God. In deference to my religious convictions (born-again animist), I don't work on Sundays. Not work-work, anyhow. Instead, I spend the morning splitting firewood—the sort of simple, honorable, invigorating, self-serving chore some call "karma" work, in that it exercises the spirit as well as the body.

And it's true. Getting in the winter's wood, like getting in the winter's wild meat—in each instance, going personally to nature to receive her gifts, then bringing them into your home and heart at the cost of your own toil and sweat—this is the way life was *meant* to be, *sculpted* thus through millions of years of pick-and-choose evolution. Without this essential, deeply personal, dirt-on-hands connection to life-giving nature, which few modern folk have the opportunity or, sadly, even the *desire* to experience these virtual-reality days—well, it's no wonder we suffer so from existential angst. Hunting and gathering (firewood, mushrooms, berries) may or may not constitute a "mystical experience," depending on your outlook, but it sure feels good in the doing, and it sure feels good when it's done. Yes, karma work indeed. For once, it wasn't Abbey who said it best, but that wise old Buddhist dog P'ang Chu-shih ...

How wondrous, how mysterious! I carry fuel, I draw water.

🦌

But where *were* we? OK ... in mid-afternoon I begin the daily transition to reality. Half an hour out, having attained the first bench, I pause to catch my breath before it escapes me completely, then join a well-trod game trail for more climbing.

Some time later I veer off the path and bushwhack out through an open forest of spruce, fir and pine, trimmed around with my favorite tree in the world, good old quaking aspen. Over the years I have on occasion spotted elk (and almost as often had them spot me) while hiking through this open stretch, yet I don't really take my comings and goings here too seriously; just another commute. Still, my line is in the water, so to speak, from the moment I step out my door, and I always move quietly and stay alert. Thus can one alone in the woods see twice as much as a talkative two.

At a rocky lip the terrain banks steeply down before leveling out on a broad aspen bench watered by a diamond-chain of small perennial springs: my private wapiti-watching Nirvana. Or it was, at least, until this summer's monsoons rolled in and floated all the elk away. Today, I figure to do something different; I'll follow the ridge a mile or so on up the mountain before dropping down onto the bench. See some seldom-seen scenery. Maybe stumble into the mysteriously missing wapiti.

I'm less than half a mile into this plan when a distant, blurry bugle, hailing from somewhere down below that lush, jungly shelf I usually haunt but skipped today, stops me like a wall. The elk have returned, if in fact they ever left.

Humming along now on a high-voltage jolt of adrenaline, I go bumbling and stumbling down the steep brushy slope, vaulting over aspen blowdown (yes, vaulting; after all I'm only fifty) and ripping my way through wild-rose tangles (nature's own concertina wire), not much worried about the racket I'm making, since the bugler is still a good piece off and elk themselves are often noisy when they move. The bull sings again and I reflect that this, August 26, is the earliest I've yet to hear serious bugling hereabouts.

I reach the shelf and slow to a fast sneak and begin a long looping approach calculated to land me just downwind of the bull—who, after sounding off a few more times in quick succession, has fallen strangely silent. Why?

After a while, even with no more bugles to guide on, I sense I'm getting close and react accordingly, halting momentarily to gauge the strength, direction and consistency of the breeze; to tune in to the subtle choir of forest sounds and reflect on what they mean; to calm and cool and sort things out. After a minute I move on, but with greater caution now, with purpose.

Just ahead, the earth swells in a stony bulge then dips and opens in a big deep gully whose bottom and near slope lie beneath my line of sight. From somewhere below the rise comes one sharp snap of limb, strengthening my suspicion that the bugler is down there; across the years I've learned to "weigh" forest sounds, and this is the sort of heavy, hard-hooved *Crack!* that almost always means elk—or, on public lands throughout the American West, perhaps a loathsome, loose-boweled beef, known locally as "slow elk." I loosen my pack, drop to my knees and crawl as close as I dare to the edge, lean out, peek over and see ...

Nothing.

Too overgrown and brushy down there to pick out any creature smaller than a brontosaurus. I wait, looking and listening. Comes another crack. And another. I worm forward—an inch, a foot— my eyes straining to see what my ears are hearing.

Suddenly, with all the grace of a seven-hundred-pound Olympic skater, a big-bodied, heavy-antlered 5x5 bull elk comes popping over the gully's lip and trots smartly across right in front of me ... and keeps on trotting. In hopes of stopping him, if even for a moment, I reach into the breast pocket of my camo shirt for a diaphragm call—a square inch of (unused) prophylactic latex stretched across a small plastic horseshoe—pop it in my mouth and blow a quick series of chirps. These terse, high-pitched, repetitive elk "I'm over here and all is well" calls, while commonly referred to as "cow" calls, and in fact most often used by cows to keep track of their calves, and vice-versa, are also made by bulls. While generally, and accurately, described as sounding like cat mews and bird chirps (to my ear, specifically the red-shafted flicker), the sound is even more reminiscent of, in fact identical to, the chirpy communication calls of Nile crocodiles. If elk and crocs shared the same habitat, there could be some interesting confusions.

The bull doesn't even so much as flick an ear at my call, but just keeps rolling along, bemused, insouciant and by now almost out of sight. How could he not have heard me? Or hearing, not have been curious enough to stop, turn and check out that alluring-sounding cow? Especially this time of year, when boy elk are crazed with that oldest and deadliest and, at the best of times, most gratifying of male diseases, testosterone poisoning.

I haven't long to wait and wonder, for now, from behind me in the gully, comes a Gatling-gun staccato of cracking limbs and thudding hooves accompanied by a chorus of chirps and mews, not unlike my own. Suddenly I'm awash in elk, a tidal wave of wapiti surging up from the gully and flooding past all around me.

The breeze here in this convoluted terrain is as unreliable as a commuter airline, and as the elk flow past I'm amazed at their collective failure to smell me. Or maybe they just don't care. They, like the bull they're following, are just goofing along, totally off-guard; the calves all prancing and dancing like colts in a spring pasture. I count six cows and six leggy calves with big faded spots still on.

I watch, awe-struck, as they come ... and go. When the last of the animals has passed—a straggling, gamboling calf who sees me and tentatively approaches, recklessly curious, before bolting away to join the others—and the herd is well out front of me, I rise and follow cautiously after, knee-crawling and cow talking as I go; just one of the girls, me. Ahead, the animals disappear by ones and pairs down into a wooded swale.

When it seems safe, I ease up a ways and stop again, watching, listening, trying to get a take on the shifty breeze, not wanting to rush in blindly and squander this golden moment. As always, my first concern when playing this ancient game is to remain undetected; to float through the forest like a ghost, alerting nothing and leaving no sign of my passing. For a twentieth-century man, his ancestral predatory skills rusted to the point of rot, it's a job of work. But fun work.

I can no longer see any elk—though not far ahead, they've disappeared into the bottom of the little valley. For a minute, all is quiet. Now comes an odd, unfamiliar sound. I'm nonplused, at a loss to guess what sort of shenanigans might be going on down there in the shadows. Certainly, it's nothing I've ever encountered before: not the hard, bony clack of antler slamming against antler; nor is it the rough grating sound of antlers "horning" a tree; neither is it any sort of elk vocalization I've ever heard, heard of or can even imagine.

Finally, incredibly, it dawns on me that what I'm hearing is a loud, enthusiastic *splashing*.

Beyond curious now, I belly up a few more feet to a clump of Gambel's oak, peek around—and there's the whole little herd, running nose to tail in a big loose loop, like cowboy-movie Indians harassing a circled wagon train. And as each of the running animals comes in turn around to a spring pool the size of a horse trough—situated just below me at the head of the depression, and the nucleus about which the animals are in dizzy orbit —it leaps gaily into the water, splashes therein briefly, then leaps back out just in time to escape being trampled by the next animal in line.

Now, here comes—and there goes—the big bull, cavorting like some overgrown calf. How I wish my camera were in my hands, rather than buried deep in my pack.

I've spent a fair piece of time living among, studying and spying on elk—almost twenty years in fact. And across all those years, I've seen some odd and interesting play behavior, particularly among calves: leaping and bucking and twisting, mock sparring, tail-chasing, head-butting and the like. But never have I seen group play so well choreographed yet wonderfully wacky as this. And it's the more remarkable yet because every least beast in the band is participating. Even the bull. In fact, it's the bull—who, this time of year, *should* be a grumpy, bossy old curmudgeon—who appears to be the instigator of it all. I love it when animals do what they *want* to, rather than what they're *supposed* to.

Wild animals at play—an enchanting, much-debated, little understood and marvelously mysterious phenomenon.

True play behavior has been documented only among higher vertebrates—suggesting, it seems, that any brainless twit can work till he (or she) drops, but it takes some smarts to kick back and enjoy life. The science of ethology—the study of animal behavior—defines play as activity that's not "in earnest." In other words, play is a luxury behavior, superfluous to survival and procreation and therefore likely to erupt only when animals are rested and relaxed and have their bellies full—which would seem to fit well with the wild scene unfolding here and now.

Traditional, conservative wildlife biology holds that a primary function of animal play is to help infant and adolescent beasts learn about their big wild world, about their own bodies and their strengths and weaknesses. Among very young animals, much and maybe most play behavior *is* no doubt motivated by instinct and directed toward developing muscular strength, co-ordination and agility—in short, vocational training: mock sparring among bull elk calves and bighorn lambs; coyote pups chasing, tackling and biting one another just as they will be required to chase, tackle and bite their prey; cougar cubs pouncing from hiding onto the necks of litter-mates, exactly as they will ambush and bring down deer as adults.

Just so.

But then—what of the yearling black bear cubs I once observed sledding down a snowy June avalanche chute on their round brown rumps, hurrying back to the top, checking in briefly with an indulgent mom, then zipping down again? And again? And what of the big boar grizzly Doug Peacock filmed cavorting in a remote Montana beaver pond; after goofing around for a while, the bear suddenly stopped and let the water go calm and glassy around him, then blew bubbles on its surface and gently pushed them around with his nose. What about that? Or the sow grizzly and alpha female wolf Caroline and I watched playing turn-about tag on a high snow drift in Yellowstone country one recent spring morning? Or the lone cow elk splashing in a shallow pond, then stopping to stare, mesmerized, at the wave circles she'd created? Where is the training value in these and a multitude of equally capricious activities regularly indulged in by mammals both young and adult?

Clearly, not all play among animals, perhaps not even the most of it, is prompted by instinct or serves any "useful"—what ethologists call "in earnest"—function. It seems inescapably obvious that elk and other "high order" wild creatures commonly play, just as do humans, *strictly for the fun of it.*

The play motive for these crazy Colorado wapiti I'm watching right now seems apparent—it's a warm, late-summer afternoon, and a dip in the old swimming hole must surely feel fine. They're enjoying a spontaneous pool party, and that big beautiful herd bull—spitting playfully in the face of the way he's "supposed" to behave during rut—is the instigator of it all.

Much too soon, of course, the bull swerves away from the circling herd, stops and stands and belches out a coarse half-bugle, then whirls and trots off down the wee wooded valley, directly away from me. He is followed, albeit reluctantly, by the cows and, finally, the cavorting calves, the latter still leaping and dodging and bucking as they go.

As quickly as they came, the elk are gone.

Feeling suddenly very alone, and for no good reason that occurs to me—other, perhaps, than the sheer, joyful hell of it; play behavior, if you will—I whistle up a couple of pretty-good fake bugles. I'm not in the least surprised when the departing bull doesn't bother to rebut my impudent insult.

Like me, he obviously doesn't work on Sundays.

What's in a Name?

WHAT'S IN A NAME?

Wily old Willy the Shake, through the star-crossed lips of lovely young Juliet Capulet, posed that rhetorical query centuries ago. But here in the American West today, the same question bears on a complex confusion involving elk, commercial elk ranching and state wildlife managers. On its surface it's a nominal question, and at least twice before we thought we had it all figured out — elk speciation, that is. Then came the recent rampant rage for the commercialization of wildlife, erupting like a pox and prompting the Colorado Division of Wildlife, for one, to take a closer look at what's in the name *Cervus elaphus*.

Specifically: Are Eurasian red deer and North American wapiti the same beast, or no? And either way, what does the categorical lumping of these two continentally segregated deer mean in the modern, pragmatic world of wildlife management?

Locally, the unrest started some years ago, when wildlife managers began taking note of the problems that arose after mouflon sheep were introduced to the wild in a couple of locations here in Colorado, and mouflon and other exotic big game species were turned loose in New Mexico ... problems such as the exotics carrying disease to native wildlife, the exotics out-competing the natives for habitat, the exotics interbreeding with the natives. And more. In the end, which didn't take that long in coming, the Colorado Division of Wildlife had to exterminate the troublesome

11

moufs. New Mexico, meanwhile, is still struggling with various exotic problems of their own making.

Thus alerted to the biological quagmire attendant to exotics, Colorado wildlife authorities turned their attention to elk, alarmed by the increasing number of red deer being imported into the country, and the state, by a fledgling but aggressive elk ranching industry. In 1982, Colorado had issued only seventy-five "commercial wildlife park" permits; by 1991, the number had tripled to 225.

A primary concern was that sooner or later some of the immigrant red deer were bound to escape from their fenced paddocks into the wild, where they would enthusiastically interbreed with Colorado's indigenous Rocky Mountain elk. Granted, contemporary Colorado wapiti are overwhelmingly the descendants of Yellowstone elk brought here early in the century to replenish the state's own decimated natives; yet the old and new are biologically identical and thus, in effect, indigenous.

Nor, in retrospect, was this needless paranoia. According to Canadian ungulate expert Valerius Geist, "Between 1989 and 1992, game ranchers in Colorado reported the escape of 231 elk and red deer, of which fifty-two, including thirty-one red deer, were never recaptured. Between 1992 and 1994, hybrids of elk and red deer were discovered in Colorado, Wyoming and Montana."

Aggravating the state's disquiet about the possibility of red deer contaminating the indigenous wapiti gene pool was the fact that red deer stags are gung-ho rutters that can generally dominate and edge out wapiti bulls, even those much larger than themselves, in competition for cows. Thus, reckoned Division biologists, the potential existed for escaped red deer stags to foul the genetics of the native elk population far out of proportion to their numbers.

Consequently, proscriptive legislation was enacted and, since July of 1990, it has been illegal to trade in red deer in Colorado or to import them into the state. Idaho seems on the verge of enacting similar restrictions, and other western elk states may well follow; Wyoming has long had an across-the-board ban on game "farming" (a trend that needs to spread).

It's in light of such recent troublesome developments in elk bio-politics that many interested observers are left wondering: What's in a name? All this talk of "foreigners" and "exotics" and "diluting gene pools" would appear to contradict contemporary biological taxonomy, which states flatly that Eurasian red deer and North American wapiti ("white rump" in Shawnee) are members of the same species, the latter technically a subspecies of the former. Thus is the question raised: If red deer and wapiti are in fact the same species, then what difference would it make if they *were* to interbreed?

Little, or so it would seem at first, maybe even second glance. After all, how can both sides of the same coin be face-up at once? Some doubting Toms, commercial wildlife ranchers for the most part of course, have even commented that perhaps Colorado should rescind its prohibition against red deer. That, or else taxonomists—those necessarily pedantic biologists whose job it is to classify all living things into species and assign scientific names—should rethink their position and separate red deer and wapiti into separate species (as once they had been).

Fueling the confusion is the fact that, through a sophisticated form of blood testing known as serum protein electrophoresis, science now can discern genetically between red deer and wapiti. Send the Analytical Genetics Testing Lab in Denver (or the Wyoming Diagnostics Lab at the University of Wyoming, or the Saskatoon Bovine Research Council in Canada) a few drops of "elk" blood and they can tell you—using triple-redundant tests with an accuracy of 1:8000 or better—whether that blood came from a red deer, a wapiti or a hybrid of the two.

What science *can't* tell us, and may never be able to tell us, is from which of the four currently recognized North American elk "subspecies" a blood sample was drawn—this, primarily because there likely *are* no genetic differences in the four. According to Val Geist and a growing number of other authorities, North America has but *one* elk subspecies, *C. e. canadensis*.

All of this leads some observers to maintain that—based on current scientific evidence that the Eurasian and North American variations of genus *Cervus* are genetically distinct—they should be reclassified as separate species.

There's more than enough confusion here to warrant a closer look at this nominal quandary. And the place to begin, I reckon, is the beginning.

In the beginning.

Which is to say, quite a long while ago, way back when the Cervidae, or deer family, were hot into the process of evolving themselves into the various species of artfully antlered, high-wired wildings we know and love today—somewhere along in there, farther back in time than the myopic human mind can comprehend—elk appeared as a distinct genus (*Cervus*): smaller than moose, but larger than deer and caribou. Like so many other bio-beginnings, that little drama most likely unfolded in central Asia, perhaps at the broad green feet of the haughty Himalayas.

In time, numbers of these prototypical elk spread westward, across endless Asia and on into Europe, adapting to local conditions—climate, habitat, predators—as they went, evolving minor differences in morphology (physical appearance) and behavior. These were and are the red deer—the archetypal species of modern elk (*Cervus elaphus elaphus*).

Meanwhile, other early elk drifted north and east from their place of genesis, beyond Lake Baikal (the likely origin area of the first "native" American immigrants), adapting incrementally to tougher winters, taller mountains and treeless tundra grasslands (steppes) as they worked their way through Mongolia and the Siberian Uplands, onto the Chukchi Peninsula and, at long last, to the ephemeral Asian-American land link of Beringia.

Beringia, a palpable Pacific version of the mythical Lost Atlantis—known also as the Bering-Chukchi Platform and (a misleading and largely antiquated term) the Bering Land Bridge—was a low, treeless, thousand-mile-deep (north to south) land mass (some "bridge," eh?) exposed when swelling glaciers trapped enough of Earth's water to significantly lower sea levels. This was all awhile back, of course, during the Illinoian (180,000 to 120,000 years ago) and Wisconsin (55,000 to 10,000 years ago) glacial stages at the butt-end of the good old Pleistocene epoch.

Across its erratic career (up and down, up and down), Beringia provided a mammoth terrestrial tie between Asia and Alaska—essentially, the whole huge area that today is inundated by the shallow East Siberian and Chukchi seas, including of course the Bering Strait and, on the west, everything from the tip of the Alaskan Peninsula to the Anadyr Gulf of the Chukchi Peninsula—in effect, a low-lying subcontinent (check it out on a map; you'll be amazed). The elk that adapted to Beringian life and were shaped by that adaptation, being literally lodged in the lurch between Asia and America, were the forebears of modern American *and* Siberian/Mongolian wapiti.

The oldest elk remains yet discovered in North America date to the Illinoian glacial period, no longer ago than 120,000 years. When the glaciers melted and lifted the seas and Beringia "sank" like Atlantis—along about nine to twelve thousand years ago—the wapiti subspecies of elk/red deer was geographically cleaved into Asian and North American branches. Consequently, as Valerius Geist points out, wapiti on both sides of the Bering Strait yet look the same, sound the same, behave the same and even stink the same. They *are* the same.

To restate: All modern Eurasian red deer and all modern North American wapiti share the same species (in bio-speak, they are "conspecific"), but different subspecies, with the wapiti being a subspecies of red deer, not vice versa. Furthermore, both Siberian and American wapiti, having shared the same habitat and genes as recently (to employ a convenient median) as ten thousand years ago, are members of the same subspecies as well as the same species.

As an avid student of both elk and early man (and, of course, wo-man), I find it invigorating to realize that toward the end of Beringia's most recent rise to dry-land fame (not likely its last, unless of course global warming gets entirely out of hand), wapiti and ancestral "native Americans" drifted toward, occupied and eventually "crossed the bridge" together. (The humans, perhaps, following the wapiti?) Thus, there may be no more ancient man-beast relationship on our continent than the multi-millennial, predator-prey blood brotherhood of "American" Indians and "American" wapiti—neither of which, in point of fact, is native to this continent by evolutionary origin.

Nor has anything really changed all that much since then. Just as Siberian and North American wapiti (and moose, and brown bears, etc.) remain physically indistinguishable, so do the Siberian and Alaskan Eskimos.

When wapiti arrived in Alaska, they wasted no time fanning south and east, eventually occupying virtually every habitable niche across the continent, Pacific to Atlantic, and south all the long way to central Mexico. Meanwhile, Alaska grew colder and finally froze out as elk habitat. The wapiti, hardy and lucky, had run the glacial gauntlet just in time.

And once here, they multiplied like lagomorphs. According to the calculations of the widely respected early twentieth-century naturalist Ernest Thompson Seton—heaven knows how accurate they are, but they're rarely disputed, broadly accepted and, in the end, all we've got—some ten million wapiti populated the New World at the time Christopher Columbus washed ashore.

And we know what happened next: European (human) emigrants out-bred and out-gunned America's elk and other wildlife to the point that by 1922 only a paltry ninety thousand or so wapiti survived, nearly half of those huddled within the marginally protective bounds of Yellowstone Park in Wyoming and Montana.

It was then, feeling America's collective disgrace at scraping the bottom of the wildlife barrel, that hunter-conservationist Theodore Roosevelt, aided by an influential handful of like-minded others, stepped to the fore to save the day just before dark.

Today, slouching anxiously into a new century, a new millennium, North America is blessed with nearly a million elk, most of which roam the Rockies in the lower forty-eight, with roughly a quarter of the lot lodged right here in Colorado.

🌿

Throughout the formative decades of biological science—that is, prior to the mid-1700s—taxonomic anarchy reigned. Every time someone discovered a new species of plant or animal, it was named largely according to whim, given that no universally accepted system of scientific nomenclature existed. Consequently, biologists working independently sometimes discovered the same creature virtually simultaneously—*bang-bang*—but, each being ignorant of the other, assigned conflicting names. With more biologists hitting the fields every year and more new species consequently being discovered and capriciously named, and feuds breaking out over which of two or more redundant names had priority—well, this just couldn't be allowed to continue, not in the (ideally) well-ordered world of biological science.

Finally, in 1758, Swedish biologist Carl von Linné—better known today by his self-inflicted "scientific" name, Carolus

Linnaeus—published the tenth edition of his *Systema Naturae*, in which he introduced a system of biological taxonomy that quickly became accepted as *the* system of biological taxonomy.

Linnaeus's no-nonsense approach employed just two words, drawn primarily from Latin but also from classical Greek, to describe a living thing. Why, it's fair to wonder, did crafty Carl opt for this pair of long-dead, tongue-twisting languages? Simply and reasonably to avoid international fusses over perceived favoritism to any living language, as with the preponderance of German terms in the field of glacial geology.

The first word in a Linnaean species name, italicized and capitalized, identifies the animal's genus—*Homo* ("man"); the second word, italicized but lower-cased, is the species identifier (technically, "specific epithet")—*sapiens* ("wise"). A third word, when it appears, signifies subspecies, if such exists, and goes around dressed in italics but uncapitalized.

Among the first species Linnaeus named using this system was *Cervus* (Latin for "stag") *elaphus* (from the Greek *elaphos* for "deer"). The father of taxonomy—with what some observers of the time no doubt saw as presumptive bravura—declared *Cervus elaphus* to include not just the several subspecies of Eurasian red deer, but the six (at the time) living "subspecies" of North American wapiti as well. Thus, from the very beginning, red deer and wapiti were lumped into the same species.

Linnaeus's *Systema* worked smoothly for a while, but before even a century had passed, under the weight of some four hundred thousand newly discovered species (mostly insects) and with more crawling into scientific awareness every day, the *Systema* began to wobble like a camel with a terminal load of straw on its back. Consequently, in 1889, a group of scientists met in Holland to form an International Congress of Zoology—and among their first functions was to appoint an International Commission on Zoological Nomenclature. And to this new Zoo Crew went the formidable task of straightening out the kinky biological taxonomics mess.

Progress was slow, hampered by squabbles among biologists who wanted their own species names to dominate over names assigned by the competition. But the ICZN persisted, and eventually triumphed. To sort out the problem of nominal redundancy, the commission instituted a "law of priority," which states that the first name assigned to a species and recorded under the Linnaean system has priority over later names. Simple, what?

To spell out its goals and keep track of its progress, the ICZN published a code of taxonomic standards, the *Regles Internationales de Nomenclature Zoologique,* or simply *Regles.* Only in 1961 was the venerable old *Regles* superseded by the current International Code of Zoological Nomenclature.

So, at first and for more than a century, it was accepted that red deer and wapiti were conspecifics. Then, in 1870, a small but influential cadre of biologists who disagreed with Linnaeus finally fought their way to the fore. The gist of their argument was that sufficient physical differences existed between the two—the wages of some ten thousand years of continental, and therefore genetic, segregation—to justify splitting waps and reds into separate species. It's a tenacious and tangy biological controversy, this tiff between "lumpers," who pull to combine species, and "splitters," who agitate to separate established conspecifics.

With Linnaeus no longer around to defend himself, the arguments of the splitters became widely if not universally accepted, at which point the wapiti's specific epithet was changed from *C. elaphus* to *C. canadensis* (Latin for "of Canada"), designating it a species apart from the Eurasian red deer, which plodded on as *elaphus.*

For the next seven decades, the wapiti's all-American status stuck, endorsed even by such biological luminaries as Olaus Murie. Then, in the early 1950s, things came full circle when a trio of renowned lumpers challenged the nominal separation of reds and wapiti, holding that Linnaeus had been right from the get-go. In 1982, this lumper view was codified in the contemporary elk scholar's bible, *Elk of North America: Ecology and Management,* and it seemed that the matter was finally settled. According to that tumescent tome:

> The existing evidence is in favor of considering the Eurasian red deer and the North American elk as a single species. Since the specific name *elaphus* ... has priority over *canadensis* ... the North American elk will be accepted as *Cervus elaphus.*

But such a lively polemic as this dies hard, if ever, in the combative scientific community, and the odd brave splitter still occasionally rears his stubborn head to lobby for American independence. In my wholly unscientific, first-ever book, *Among the Elk,* I summarized these common-sense contentions:

> The splitters argue that differences in body size (the wapiti is larger than the red deer), coloration, voice, antler size and configuration, geographical location and length of separation are more than sufficient to establish the two as distinct species.

Sounds good, and until recently, I'll admit I had a splitter tilt myself. But after tracking down and wrestling with the facts—when all else fails, read the instructions—I was finally and firmly co-opted to the lumper team.

Here's why: For centuries, biological speciation was determined primarily by the morphological approach, which involved measuring and comparing physical, especially skeletal, features. More recently, the larger "phylogenetic"—that is, evolutionary or racial history—speciation approach has assumed dominance. Which, of course, changes things.

By and large, the morphological view of speciation leads to something of a stand-off when applied to *C. elaphus.* Examine a red deer stag alongside a bull wapiti, and whether the "evidence" your senses gather suggests lumping or splitting depends in large part on how you choose to interpret what you see, hear and smell. Granted, the two big deer look strikingly alike, outside and in. Yet, there are obvious physical distinctions. For example: the rutting stag's throaty, deep-woods "roar" versus the wapiti's shrill, long-range "whistle."

The second—phylogenetic, or evolutionary—approach treats morphology as but one among several elements in species determination. For an instance: Geological and fossil records testify that the Eurasian red deer and our own beloved wapiti have been salt-water segregated by an unswimmable (for most of us) ocean strait, fifty-six miles wide at its narrowest, for around ten thousand years. And this, of course, proves ...

Well, nothing, in fact. As with physical distinctions, the time of separation of red deer and wapiti is offered as "evidence" to bolster the arguments of both schools. While splitters hail a continental separation of ten millennia as plenty long enough—evidenced by observable differences in external physical appearances and male vocalizations—to justify severing wapiti from red deer, lumpers refer to the same span as "an exceedingly short period of geological time," insufficient to allow significant genetic change.

Alas, in the final shake-down, the temporal argument is little more than intellectual gainsaying. The big gun in the phylogenetic arsenal is the fact that red deer and wapiti are capable of breeding and producing fertile offspring—bad news for splitters, in that this knack is generally accepted as a, even *the*, primary species marker.

What, then, of electrophoresis and its ability to discern genetically between red deer and wapiti, but not between North American ecotypes? Doesn't this provide rich fodder for the splitters? Well, I sort of thought maybe so—until I spoke with the experts at Colorado's Analytical Genetics Testing Lab.

The learned white-coats there listened patiently to my convoluted query, then gently explained that the ability to differentiate
genetically between red deer and wapiti indicates only that
enough time has passed in mutual isolation for evolution to have
begun shaping genetic differences in the two. No more. No less.
Electrophoretic genetic differentiation, they warned, should *not*
be interpreted as an indication of a definitive splitting of the
species.

Thus, the phylogenetic bottom line remains unchanged by
electrophoresis—and, for that matter, by DNA research: only
when two groups of former conspecifics have been geographically separated sufficiently by time *and* environment to allow
them to have evolved far enough apart so that they can no longer
interbreed and produce fertile offspring, only then can they properly be considered to be separate species. Such, at least, is current
policy, and reds and wapiti fail that seminal test.

So now, finally, we approach the end of this tortuous track
only to find ourselves smack back at the trail-head facing the
same old question: If red deer and wapiti are, beyond any rea-
sonable doubt, one and the same species—as science presently
swears up and down they are—then why are Colorado wildlife
managers so adamant about maintaining the "genetic purity" of
our Rocky Mountain elk?

Because they, and the public they represent, perceive the wapiti
as a grander beast—a sentiment with which I agree.

How are red deer less grand than wapiti? In at least four quan-
tifiable aspects: body size, body weight, antler mass and quality
of vocalization. "Bigger is better" is an American cliché, and
likewise, we can predict a strong continental preference for the
traditional screaming bugle over the foreign foghorn blast of rutting red deer stags. Thus does the Colorado Division of Wildlife
reason that should even a few feral red deer hybridize with
Rocky Mountain wapiti to the point that body and antler size in

the state's wild elk should diminish—even a little, even only in isolated geographical pockets—and (worse yet) should instances of this hybridization be proven by electrophoresis and publicized in the national sporting media, nonresident hunters (it is perceived) would stay away in droves.

"So what?" asks the nonhunting majority, adding, many of them, "Good riddance!"

So, since the Colorado Division of Wildlife, like all state wildlife agencies, depends heavily on the sale of big game hunting licenses for its operational funding—pricey nonresident elk tags are the Division's single largest source of income—any significant loss in the number of elk hunters would hurt where it hurts most: in the purse. Consequently, the ability to manage the state's wildlife—and, more importantly, to manage the people who otherwise would negatively affect our wildlife—would be seriously diminished, introducing a downward spiraling trend. Or so, at least, it is officially perceived.

In the end, it seems that Colorado has answered, at least to its own satisfaction and mine, the question: "What's in a name?" with the response: "Exactly what we want there to be."

Ultimately, Colorado's decision to oust red deer from America's leading elk state was influenced not one whit by the current preference of biological taxonomy. Rather, it was motivated—arguably *necessitated* —by the entrenched conception among many hunters that bigger is better, by perceived fiscal imperative, by good old-fashioned national pride ... and, most admirably, by a wholesome and genuine desire to preserve ten thousand years of hard evolutionary work.

Postscript: After reading a draft of the above, a perceptive friend from the professional wildlife management community posed the logical question: "That's all well and good when we're talking about red deer, but what if some of the Roosevelt's elk that game ranchers are bringing into Colorado (from the Pacific Northwest) should escape and mingle with the Rocky Mountain natives; wouldn't that pose similar problems of identity? Why prohibit red deer but allow Roosevelt's?"

Good question.

And like all good questions, it leads to several others. For a few examples: Does the larger-bodied and smaller-antlered Roosevelt's *(Cervus elaphus rooseveltii)* ecotype threaten the "classic" Rocky Mountain elk's genetic identity? And if so, should not captive importation of not just red deer, but the Roosevelt's and other non–Rocky Mountain wapiti be outlawed in Colorado and the other Rocky Mountain elk states?

And ultimately: Where (and why) should such well-meaning, perhaps necessary but impossibly tangled proscriptive legislation start and stop?

The dominant opinion, as expressed in *Elk of North America* and elsewhere, is that America presently has four geographically isolated elk populations, each sufficiently distinct from the others to justify subspecies designation. But a challenging and clearly more logical viewpoint—Geist et al., previously mentioned—holds that all North American wapiti should be lumped together as just one collective subspecies under the scientific heading *Cervus elaphus canadensis*. According to Geist, writing in the Fall 1990 issue of *Bugle*:

> Are the Tule elk of California not different from the Rocky Mountain elk in Wyoming or the Roosevelt's elk on the Olympic Peninsula? They are different, of course, but they differ in ways governed by the ecological conditions they live in, not the genes they carry. We are concerned far less with subspecies than with different ecotypes that reflect the food, seasons and climate—the

opportunities and liabilities of the land they live in. Put elk behind a fence and a hay crib year-round and see if anybody can
guess where they originally came from. Give Tule elk runts three
square meals a day and watch what happens!

Strengthening this lumper stance, remember, is the fact that genetic testing presently cannot distinguish between any of the four
currently classified "subspecies." This, in turn, suggests that gene
flow between the four geographically segregated types has not
been interrupted long enough to make any noticeable (pheno-
typical) difference.

Whether you accept the single-subspecies idea or not, the Colorado Division of Wildlife does. Having anticipated this logical
extension of the red deer controversy, the Division gave the question some thought and decided that no, the other three regional
types of North American elk do not pose a threat to the genetic
purity of Colorado's natives. Should a few captive Roosevelt's escape into the wild and interbreed with the locals, any physical
differences in the hybrid offspring will, after a very few generations—like so many General MacArthurs—just fade away. The
Division felt that a line must be drawn somewhere, and chose to
draw it at the level of continental separation.

Well, good on the Division. Yet, were I given the power and the
pen, I'd draw the line at the root of all such concerns by outlaw-
ing elk "ranching" altogether, on the grounds that it's a cruel, de-
meaning and grossly inappropriate "use" of such grand wild creatures as wapiti, and a proven health threat—to wild elk, domestic
livestock and even humans—when escapees transmit diseases (including especially Bovine Tuberculosis) to wild populations; or,
working in reverse, when some elk "farmer" intentionally opens
his pasture gates and allows, even lures, wild wapiti in to bolster
his diseased captive herd. Tragically, control of wildlife ranching
in Colorado, as has been the case in other states, recently was

wrested from the Division of Wildlife and handed to the state agricultural department, that most churlish, insular and destructive of all government agencies, IRS, FBI, CIA, ATF and MiB notwithstanding.

Ah, but we're straying into a whole 'nuther forest of trees here, best saved for another chapter's chopping.

Among the Elk
and the Aspens

The fine leaves of the aspens, delicately suspended, shimmered like water under light, shivered and tinkled like glass bells with the slightest breeze, and their rustling taken all together resembled the whispering of voices, murmurs, speech without words.
—Edward Abbey

A GOLDEN SEPTEMBER MORNING.

It was hours ago that I wedged myself out of bed, got dressed in a woodsy way, drank some coffee, munched some cereal, stepped out the cabin door, hopped in the truck, drove up the road and enjoyed the stiff steep walk through star-spangled darkness that brought me to this special place before the first yawn of dawn.

A job of work it was, always is, but worth every panting breath, every drop of sweat, every minute's sleep lost.

I have come here, as on so many mornings and evenings before, in search of elk. Sometimes I find them. More often I don't. Either way, there is no place on this lovely Earth I'd rather be in autumn, nothing I would rather be doing, than hanging out on some rocky old mountainside, in some lovely old grove of quaking aspens, watching and listening.

Watching—you know what for, though just now, in the predawn darkness, only the few nearest chalk-white quakie trunks are visible, like a gathering of gaunt forest ghosts.

27

And listening—for the speech without words that will come when the morning thermals stir the loose-jointed, fall-brittle leaves of the quakies all around me. And, of course, for the lustful screams of rutting wapiti, like bent high notes on a bluesy saxophone.

But this day, as on so many others, the first morning sounds are neither elk bugles nor whispering aspens, but a pair of pine squirrels thrashing about in dry leaves, screaming their ratchety territorial calls. Sometimes, I've noticed, these raspy pronouncements are followed by a series of sing-song chirps that remind me—in miniature but precisely—of the post-bugle "chuckles" of rutting bull elk.

The sun finally drags itself above the eastern skyline, fingers through the mixed aspens and conifers (pine, spruce, Dougfir and fir) and winks itself awake in the little spring pool just below my hillside perch. With the warm, welcome light comes a raucous parade of birds—a big, cocky, black-tipped gray Clark's nutcracker; a scattering of scolding Steller's jays in waistcoats of midnight blue; a few hopping juncos; a brace of tiny nuthatches; a single, sweet-voiced chickadee—all flocking to the spring for a drink and, sometimes, a bath, understandably quick in the deep dawn chill.

Time passes.

The morning, though still young, has grown warm and bright before the first elk announces its approach. Not with brash bugles but much more subtly than that: a hollow echoing knock, like a horse's hoof striking deadfall; a rhythmic crunching, far too solid and heavy to be a squirrel, through the yellow leaves; one sharp *Pop!* of breaking limb. Big animal. Moving boldly. Coming in to water.

I raise my camouflage face net, take a deep breath and fix my attention, my entire being, on the spot where the game trail opens into a small clearing just behind the spring.

A few moments more and a big dark head and bright white antlers appear. Big antlers; not exceptionally heavy, but wide and long-tined, six to the side. This lonely character, I reckon, must be the senior satellite bull on the mountain just now. So deep into the rut as this, a herd bull would not be here alone, without his harem. My heart races and my mouth goes dry and I wonder if I'm trembling from two long hours of sitting still as a stone in the sharp morning cold—or from something more ancient and visceral.

The bull, big as a small horse, has stopped at the edge of the aspens, instinctively cautious, checking things out. As well he should.

Morning thermals stir intermittent zephyrs that set the quakies humming with a dry, brittle music, not unlike a Navajo gourd rattle. Just the thing to conceal the tom-tom beating of my heart. This is the moment I wait all year, every year, to experience—just me and the wapiti, alone together, among the aspens.

Aspens and elk. Elk and aspens. The two go together like—what? Choose your cliché.

Elk and aspens. Aspens and elk. Aesthetically as actually, each enriches the other.

While the ranges of Rocky Mountain elk and quaking aspens are similar throughout the West, they aren't identical. Heavy concentrations of elk sometimes are found in areas having few or no aspens—such as much of northern Idaho and Montana. And in the East, of course, stand sprawling aspen groves no longer blessed by the brassy bugling of elk—our forefathers and Manifest Destiny saw to that. But where the ranges of elk and aspens are sympatric, or overlapping, the quakie forest—which can be all-white or intermixed with conifers—is heaven on Earth for elk.

Why do elk seek out the aspens?

In a word, *habitat*. In two words, *quality* habitat.

Elk require only four gifts from the land: nutritious and varied forage; clean, perennial water; cover thick and expansive enough to hide them from their enemies (humans most especially included) and to provide a modicum of shelter from sun, wind and inclement weather; and plenty of room to roam. The western quaking aspen ecology provides all these basics, and something more: I like to think that wapiti, and other wildlife as well, appreciate the *ambiance* of the aspens, the magical *mood* these ancient groves bestow upon all who enter. All who enter, that is, with eyes and hearts open.

Aspens have been around for a good long while—somewhere in the neighborhood of fifteen million years. They belong to the willow family and the poplar genus, and wear the scientific name *Populus tremuloides*—"trembling poplars." The aspen's closest relative is the cottonwood. While members of the birch genus superficially resemble aspen, particularly so the white-barked "paper" birch of the north, the two are in no way related.

Down here in southwestern Colorado (world-champ aspen country), we affectionately call them "quakies." Old-line Montanans prefer "quakers." Meanwhile, artless "wise users" everywhere call aspens "trash trees" and see in them only pulp, particle-board and profit.

The aspen (four subspecies total) is the most widespread hardwood on earth. Moreover, the quaking aspen is the most ubiquitous tree native to North America and the only upland hardwood in many parts of the American West.

In the eastern U.S., *P. tremuloides* sprouts up from New England as far south as Virginia, is common throughout the Great Lakes states and widespread but spotty across the northern Midwest. Out West, they're a familiar and welcome sight along almost the entire length of the Rockies, from Alaska and Canada as far south as southern Arizona and New Mexico. Even below the border, down (not too far down) in Baja California and the northern states of Old Mexico, rare cool stands of tenacious quakies persist.

The two United States blessed with the greatest glory of aspens, far and away, are Colorado (particularly here on the wet Western Slope) and Utah (it's not all dusty desert and stony canyons).

Throughout the Rockies, quakers prefer south-facing subalpine slopes, where they prosper in huge pure stands, occasionally blanketing entire mountainsides. But aspen groves often as not are "invaded" (a forester's term, not mine) by ponderosa pine in the lower reaches and spruce, fir and Dougfir higher up. These mixed aspen-evergreen forests, with patches of brushy Gambel's oak sprinkled here and there, provide the finest elk habitat on earth.

In fact, it has been written, and likely is true, that aspens are more important to more species of wildlife than all other trees combined. In addition to elk, a few of the multitude of wild creatures common to the aspens include mule deer, whitetail and moose; bighorn sheep; jackrabbit (in fact a hare), cottontail and snowshoe; six species of squirrel; bears both black and grizzly; all three of North America's great wild cats; wolf, coyote and three species of fox (not counting my little Caroline); wolverine, martin and other weasels (not counting myself); beaver; porcupine; blue grouse, band-tailed pigeon, wild turkey and dove. To name but a few.

For elk, especially, the aspen ecology is a year-round commissary. The aspen understory comprises some three hundred species of grasses, brush and forbs (nongrass graze plants, including especially wildflowers), all of which prosper within the cool clean shade of the groves. Across a single summer, this understory ecology is capable of producing approximately one ton of high-quality forage *per acre*—roughly the equivalent of healthy grasslands, and about ten times the understory production of evergreen forest.

Additionally, the straight white trees themselves are an always-important, sometimes-critical food source for the giant deer. In fact, *Elk of North America* names the quaking aspen as the single most important year-round forage tree for elk, rating it as "valuable" during summer and "very valuable" during fall, winter and spring.

Across the green months, though elk are by preference grazers, they nonetheless browse the buds, twigs and leaves of aspen. And for good reason: One U.S. Forest Service study found the fat content of aspen leaves to average 7 percent in June, 8 percent in July and 10 percent in September—while protein content averaged 17 percent in June, 13 percent in July and 12 percent in September. Good stuff. Further, aspen browse is highly digestible (assuming you're a multi-stomached ungulate). Even the bark is an amazing 39 to 50 percent digestible, varying with location and season.

Given its singular attractiveness, you might expect to see overgrazing of aspen and aspen understory by elk. But it's rarely a problem, especially when compared to livestock. It's cattle and sheep, particularly the latter, that do the greatest damage to spring, summer and fall aspen saplings and summer understory. According to the U.S. Forest Service publication, *Aspen: Ecology and Management in the Western United States*:

> Wild animals shift from browse to herbaceous plants during summer. This shift to succulent food occurs when these animals usually are scattered over their summer range, making their impact on the forage resource minimal to moderate, and often not even measurable. In contrast, many domestic livestock are allowed to graze on aspen-covered ranges during the peak of the

growing season. They commonly use at least 50 percent of the annual production of palatable forage. ...

Then comes winter.

The extent of elk dependence on aspen in winter is determined largely by whether or not the range has been grazed during the warmer months by livestock, and to what extent. If no or only light livestock grazing has occurred, palatable grasses, forbs and brush will remain in cold storage beneath the snow, taking much of the elk-foraging pressure off the trees. If, however, as is far too often the case, the aspen understory has been stripped clean by livestock, and the quakie saplings chewed down to nubs, elk may be forced by starvation to gnaw aspen bark. Although it's far from the top of the wapiti's preferred foods list, the soft, living inner bark of the quaking aspen has a nutritional value approaching that of grass hay, and is often a late-winter lifesaver. Emergency rations.

Why do elk consume aspen bark and not the bark of other trees?

The aspen's soft, smooth skin is capable of limited photosynthesis—the process of converting sunshine to chlorophyll, God's own sugar, which normally is handled by the green leaves of summer—even during winter. Consequently, aspen bark is softer, moister, more palatable, digestible and nutritious than that of other trees. This is doubly so in winter, since inner aspen bark stays perennially green.

It's this soft, nutritious inner layer that elk are after when they "bark" aspens in winter. With living, standing trees, the damage is generally limited; elk rarely girdle a live aspen, removing the bark all the way around and thereby dooming the tree to slow starvation and certain death. Instinctively, they know better. With limited barking, in time, the shallow wounds blacken, swell and harden. All is healed.

The only potential for serious damage to arise from limited elk barking of mature aspens is the chance that decay organisms may enter through the wounds before healing can occur. Most often, though, no lasting harm is done and the tooth marks—along with larger, deeper gashes resulting from antler rubbing by elk and deer, as well as the long, deep, half-moon marks cut by the claws of climbing black bears and porcupines, plus the occasional egoistic graffiti carved by people with knives in their hands and air in their heads—the scars resulting from all such abuses and more, comprise a distinct aspect of aspen grove aesthetics: the writing on the bark, as it were.

With recently fallen live aspens—blowdown—winter-hungry elk exercise no such restraint and may excoriate entire trunks of accessible bark. And why not?

Notwithstanding all of this, the aspen forests see the heaviest elk use—not during the snow months, when the majority of wapiti migrate to milder elevations below the aspen belt; nor in summer, when the big herbivorous herds seek the high, cool, relatively insect-free timberline parks—but in late spring, as the hungry animals work their way slowly back up from winter to summer habitat.

My cabin squats at eight thousand feet, smack in the middle of the local aspen zone and midway between elk wintering and summering grounds. Consequently, on our daily walks, Caroline and I enjoy a bonus of wapitoid sightings during late May and early June—which, happily for us, coincides with elk-calving season.

For elk, the quakie woods provide a ready-made nursery. The grove's rich and varied understory cover, interspersed with grassy cloistered clearings, provides a bounty of secluded ecotone (edge) habitat. Jungles of deadfall and the rugged broken terrain frequented by aspens offer ample hiding cover. And where shallow-rooted quakies grow, surface water is rarely lacking. Glimpsing newborn elk calves, as we do virtually every spring—all legs and spots and fuzzy fur—is a special gift of the aspens.

Long live the quakies ... but how to assure it?

How can our public aspen forests best be managed—for their own good as well as for the benefit of elk and other wildlife and a majority of Americans with our myriad needs and wants?

Most often, the answer is to manage *ourselves*; to leave nature *alone*. One veteran Forest Service land manager confided to me (revealing an opinion contrary to his agency's proven preference) that he considers the best overall management philosophy for healthy aspen forests is to allow the trees to mature, die, fall and rot. Naturally. This, because the slow, time-release decay of deadfall maximizes the recycling of nutrients to the soil. You know—if it ain't broke, don't fix it. After all, the aspens have looked after themselves nicely for fifteen million years now.

But where aspen "treatment" is deemed "absolutely necessary" (a pair of loaded forest-industry terms open to vigorously conflicting interpretations), fire is infinitely preferable to clearcutting. While not as efficient a nutrient recycler as natural death and decay, fire nevertheless carpets the forest floor with nutrient-rich ash, which rain and melting snow dissolve and leach into the soil. Also—and a bright and shining "also" at that—burning requires no road construction.

Prescribed burning is not a holocaust, but has as its goal limited top-burning of select vegetation. The intent, and most often the result, is to cull the most combustible fuels—deadfall, snags, over-mature brush—thus purging the forest floor of accumulated ground litter that can slow the growth of new forage plants. At the same time, wise prescribed burning leaves unburnt clusters of mixed-age trees scattered here and about. After this wildfire-aping fashion, nutritious and highly palatable young growth—of aspen, brush and forbs—is encouraged, while plenty enough mature trees are left standing to provide cover and a supply of bark for winter wildlife rations.

Last and definitely least in ecological desirability is clearcutting. Unfortunately, the aspen is scorned by the forest products industry as unworthy of the cost of selective thinning. Consequently, the U.S. Forest Service endorses and even champions aspen clearcutting—in which large patches of earth are scoured of sylvan cover, the trees (and their stored nutrients) being promptly trucked away to the nearest pulp mill.

I've listened to all the arguments, read all the propaganda, stretched and strained to keep an open mind—and still can't support or even understand a philosophy that espouses destroying a forest in a purported effort to "save" it.

It is true that clearcutting stimulates aspen "suckering." Quakers regenerate primarily by pushing up saplings, or "suckers," from the roots of parent trees. Since the living top-foliage exudes a sucker-inhibiting chemical (the high-ticket term is "apical dominance"), one handy (if harsh) way to stop the flow of that chemical and enhance suckering is to amputate the tree at its base. Further, say proponents, clearcutting lets the sun in (does it ever), encouraging increased grass production.

But elk do not live by grass alone; they need the thermal protection and privacy a standing grove provides, the moisture it retains, the natural diversity of understory plants that grow only in the moist, shady company of aspens. Moreover, it's most often privately owned cattle and sheep the grass is destined for, rather than public wildlife. Finally, clearcutting destroys breathtakingly beautiful forests, leaving the land naked and flayed and scarred with roads. These new roads, in turn, invite ATV and other gas-powered abuse, resulting in radically increased harassment and poaching of elk and other wildlife, rampant littering, ruined outings for quieter, muscle-powered human visitors, etc. Finally, clearcutting cripples the natural functioning of watersheds and groundwater, and promotes devastating soil erosion.

Bottom line: Studies have shown that even when wildlife forage production does increase subsequent to clearcutting (it doesn't always), elk wisely shun the dangerously open, unpleasantly sunny, less-diverse, road-butchered and aesthetically bankrupt "cuts," clinging to the comfortable, nurturing seclusion of mature aspen groves.

Like the one I'm sitting in even now, fighting the shakes as a big bull elk approaches.

After hesitating at the far edge of the little forest clearing, a couple dozen yards to my front, the bullish beast suddenly sallies forth, headed directly for the tiny spring pool above which I hunker in hiding. But the "clearing," as with most such hiatuses in aspen groves, isn't entirely clear, and the approaching bull remains partially screened by yellow-leafed saplings and one plump young Christmas tree.

At this, the most anxious of moments, for hunters and wildlife voyeurs alike, I reassure myself that it is not to worry; every last animal that's appeared here in the past several days—a mule deer doe, several cow elk and a sleek, leggy spike bull still in velvet— has stopped and looked around, exactly as this bull is doing, then come on in to water. My reward, in every case, has been the thrill of a prolonged, close-up view—*so* close I can hear every rumble of stomach, every slurp of water going down, every sibilant fart and beat of heart (the latter being my own). This beautiful creature, cautious as he is, doubtless will do the same.

And sure enough, finally, here he comes, directly for the little pool. But almost there, almost here, still screened by brush and trees, he strikes a scent trail: a whole big slew of wapiti were in here sometime during the night—the herd bull and his harem, no doubt—leaving the earth churned with tracks, littered with droppings and spotted dark with urine. His thirst instantly forgotten, muzzle low, the bull turns and follows his nose up the hillside—the very hillside where I squat.

On he comes—fifteen yards, ten, nose to ground. Just as I'm beginning to fear he'll trample me, the bull stops and lifts his head, lifts it high, his antlers towering over me like a great bony candelabra, one dark, inscrutable eye cocked and staring suspiciously down at the odd trembling lump hunkered humbly in his path.

I dare not move, barely even risk to breathe.

After long moments of pondering my queer quivering form, the bull lets out a bark so loud it hurts my ears, rears and spins like a circus stallion and goes crashing away.

Almost instinctively, my right hand fumbles clumsily in a jacket pocket for the call. I bring it to my parched lips and bleat and mew and—by George!—the fleeing bull hauls up at the far edge of the little opening … smack back where he started from. And there he stands, head cocked around, glaring back at me over a broad left shoulder.

For seconds I'll remember always, the encounter is frozen in space and time. Then something (can't say exactly what) passes between us and the bull turns and *walks* casually away, headed back up the slope down whence he came. I don't bother trying to call him back; why trouble him further? His crunching, clomping steps soon fade, leaving me alone in a lonely aching silence.

My morning's adventure is over. No more customers are likely to show until the evening cocktail hour; no more reason to stay.

Yet, I'm in no huge hurry to abandon this forest of golden slanting light and breezy whispered voices. So I indulge a while longer in the meditation of sitting, looking, listening. Living.

Half an hour passes and I'm mentally preparing myself to leave when, from somewhere up the mountain, a bull elk issues an odd, abbreviated bugle that sounds like a yawn; he has bedded for the day and is announcing as much to the world. I take this as my signal to rise and stretch and start back down the mountain—to home and work and workaday life. How I hate to go.

Out here among the elk and the aspens, like nowhere else I know, I am at peace.

A Meditation
on Mystery

IT'S A QUIET AFTERNOON early in the rut (the wapiti's, not mine, which is fairly well advanced), and I'm slipping alone (the most lucrative way to slip) through the shivering shade of an aspen grove, when I hear a subtle ruckus somewhere ahead. I stop and point my eyes where my ears are looking, and there, a few-score yards downslope to my right, wags the big beige butt of an elk. Praise to Buddha and pass the binoculars.

Gauging the breeze by its feel on my face and judging it safe, I inch elkward, my focus locked utterly on the wapiti down the way—which, from the splashy sound of it, is either wallowing or wading in the spring pool I know to be there. My challenge, the name of this ancient game, my favorite game, is to creep cougar-close without revealing myself.

A leaning quakie looms ahead; I duck under and am just coming to vertical, surveying the ground ahead of my boots for noisy debris to dodge, when some ineffable something prompts me to look up—and there, twenty yards dead ahead, stands a beast the size, and more or less the color, of a young palomino, wearing a big hat of antlers like a nest of writing snakes. By the gods!

The splashing elk down the way is instantly forgotten in the face of this elkheart's dream come true.

For as long as I can recall—long enough that I can't recall how long—I've harbored a serious aesthetic attraction for freak, or (to be Nominally Correct) "nontypical" antlers. At every opportunity, I've admired nontypicals where they hang mounted on walls, or as photos and art. But in all that long adoring time, I've never ever been blessed with a personal close encounter. And now, posing like an apparition before my lucky eyes, is the archetypal nontypical Artiodactyla (the order of even-toed ungulates to which all deer belong). Erupting at every odd angle from high, lavishly curved main beams is a tumultuous tangle of points and hooks and nubs and knobs and myriad more shapes I lack the nouns to name.

As one who counts antlers as among evolution's grandest mysteries, nature's most wondrous works of art—right up there with birds of paradise and butterfly wings—this is an event, a moment, not to be forgot.

Antlers: a meditation on mystery. Far easier than explaining what antlers are, is to say what they are not.

Foremost, antlers are not horns. Following a long tradition of sham-ignorance honored by every rank of outdoors folk, Bubbas to biologists, I occasionally say *horn* when I really mean *antler.* This titular abuse is particularly common in casual conversation, like, "the bull elk was horning a tree." Wrong, right, but sometimes it just *sounds* better that way. In fact of course, antlers and horns are as pointedly distinct as the animals that wear them. A few for-examples:

• Only one family, the cervids, comprising four species—elk, deer, moose and caribou—have antlers. Meanwhile, three families— bovids (cattle), ovids (sheep) and caprids (goats) — have horns.

• Antlers consist of solid, dead, marrowless, mineralized bone, while horns are a composite, with a hard outer shell of keratin—the smooth shiny stuff of hair and nails—encasing a spongy living core, or matrix.

• While antlers are discarded and renewed annually, horns are for keeps. (A single exception is the all-American pronghorn, *Antilocapra americana*, which evolved on this continent and never left, has no close relatives anywhere else on earth and yearly sheds its horn sheaths, with new cases forming fast over the delicate exposed cores.)

• Each annual set of antlers is larger, more complex and spectacular than the previous year's, at least until the bull or buck is well past his breeding prime, when creeping antler atrophy sets in. Horns, meanwhile, no matter how ornately ridged, spiraled or curled, remain forever single-beamed. (Again, the solitary exception is the pronghorn, whose truly "pronged" horns have one fork.)

• While only male cervids have antlers—the single exception being caribou cows, and even then not universally across their range—both genders of horn-bearers bear horns, those of the females, not surprisingly, being quite modest alongside the often massively macho cranial appendages of the males.

Antlers are luxury organs, in that their function is social rather than physical, nonessential to the survival of the individual or of the species—this in contrast to such essential innards as, say, lungs and teeth and testicles. Only after rich forage and efficient metabolism have satisfied the nutritional needs of skeleton, muscle and gut, are the gates of possibility opened to such extravagant ornamentals as antlers.

Tracking farther along this line of logic, it follows that big antlers trumpet a triumphant triumvirate of good genes, good health and a good foraging strategy. Thus, a primary function of antlers (perhaps *the* primary function) is as social visual aids, billboards proclaiming to a cow at a glance the relative worth of the various bulls competing for her feminine flavors [*sic*].

To cows on the make, big antlers flag males who know how to find and use the best foods, who are injury- and disease- and parasite-free and who have been clever enough to survive to rutting maturity. These qualities, not coincidentally, are exactly what any competent wapiti matron instinctively craves to grant to her posterity.

Similarly, since wapiti employ a herding rut strategy—wherein the few fittest bulls hoard all the girls and good times for themselves, while subordinates are left to bugle and pout and piss and pound their inferior horns against trees—antlers serve a second essential evolutionary purpose by helping males to sort out their relative rank in the local social hierarchy. Through antler advertising, bugling, body language and instinct-choreographed sparring matches, a pecking order shakes itself down among bulls before the fact, greatly reducing the need for potentially deadly *torro e torro* tournaments during the actual rut—when, after all, dominant bulls need all their oats for other purposes.

Most animals, in fact (*Homo saps* more or less included), have evolved ways of reducing the lethality of sex-driven, hormone-fueled male dominance contests, "knowing" that to have prime breeding males killing each other off on a regular annual schedule is contrary to enhancing the weal of the species. And so it has come to pass that antlers, via billboarding, walk point for a complex strategy aimed at reducing life-and-death combat between rutting bulls.

Yet, serious rutting battles do occur. And when they do, antlers assume a tertiary role as weapons. In their design we can readily detect defensive as well as offensive elements—brow tines positioned and angled to serve as eye guards (in all deer species); shieldlike palmation (in moose and caribou); the hooking, holding and deflecting value of multiple tines raking forward from heavy main beams (in all species). Meanwhile, the pointedly *offensive* nature of antlers is obvious.

So obvious are antlers as armament, a common misconception exists that they evolved *primarily* as weapons. Certainly, antler form has been significantly shaped by and to militant ends through eons of evolution. Yet, it seems wholly unlikely that some innate, pre-existing *need* for head-mounted spears and shields was the Prime Mover of antler evolution.

If not as weapons, why *did* antlers first appear? Not likely, either, as the eye-catching marquees they are today. In their original form—slender, fuzzy, modest spikes—antlers would have served no better as visual status symbols than as weapons; all such as that would come only later. Even so, antlers likely *did* premiere as organs of sexual commerce—as *olfactory* rather than visual billboards; as scentposts rather than signposts.

It's common knowledge among experienced hunters and other woodsmen (and women) that male cervids "horn" trees and brush to facilitate the removal of tattered velvet at the conclusion of antler growth and just prior to the opening of the annual fall rut; in elk, rut begins in late August and extends through mid-October, with the majority of actual breeding going down around the first of October. Likewise, it's no secret that rutting male cervids use their racks to attack trees and brush, both to vent sexual frustration and as a nonvocal means of boasting and advertising.

Additionally, perhaps more significantly yet less commonly known, antlers are used to broadcast personal scents. Amorous bulls and bucks regularly rub scent glands, located on head and face, against trees, impregnating the bark with an oily perfume; then, in turn, scrub the antlers vigorously against the scent-impregnated bark to (re)transfer the aroma. Thus coifed, the randy dandy continues on his rounds, knowing that he's not only left his calling card at each rub site, he's also carrying it with him, publishing it on the breeze and printing it on everything he touches with his antlers as he goes along—and at just the right height to be readily detected by others of his ilk.

It's straying off the trail a bit, but worth mentioning that in a parallel olfactory advertising caper, rutting bull elk urinate into shallow water or onto muddy soil, stomp around to mix it up (stirred, not shaken), then flop down and wallow vigorously in the funky brew, paying special attention to coat and cake the heavy hairs of their neck manes. Thereafter, they tramp about rubbing their funky selves on trees and other sturdy vegetation, in this awkward but effective way broadcasting the sexy pheromones contained in their urine. While it's definitely an acquired taste, you can come to love the stout, heady stench of bull elk in rut.

Obviously, this spectacular nontypical bull browsing so casually just up the way hasn't wallowed of late, since the breeze is from him to me; were he in full-dress stench mode I'd have caught his whiff long before I saw him. But no matter: he's right there. And I'm right here, in wapiti heaven, mentally photographing every twist and turn of tine amongst those magnificently mangled horns.

Something in the human aesthetic prefers symmetry, and among antler aficionados "balance" is widely perceived as an essential element of beauty. As a natural-born contrarian, I view it all quite otherwise, seeing the greatest beauty in individual manifestations of random possibility and diversity, in the evocation of mystery. Peruse a rack of truly weird antlers and try *not* to wonder ... why, and how?

Antler anomalies are miracles within a miracle.

Genetic antler abnormalities can and do persist through generations, this "hopeful monster" scenario providing a uniquely visible example of the experimental leaps-and-bounds method by which evolution (sometimes) lurches forward. Yet, spectacular genetic aberrations appear as a distinct minority compared to a plethora of lesser antler abnormalities spawned by circumstance.

The most common, and generally the least radical headgear anomalies result from minor injuries to delicate formative antlers. At the apogee of their three- to four-month annual growth cycle, elk antlers can elongate by an inch every two days. During this frenetic period, any hard knock, against a tree or somesuch, can break a soft slender tine, or even a sturdy but brittle (not yet ossified) main beam. Most often when this happens, the protective, nourishing skin, called velvet, serves as something of a splint, holding the broken portion loosely in place, preventing its full detachment. Often, such a break heals at an awkward angle, like a poorly set bone, and is obvious in the finished antler. In those instances when a broken antler fails to mend, the affected appendage falls off when the velvet is shed, leaving in its place a definitive stump. Should an injury cleanly amputate a portion of an antler during early growth, a new tip may sprout in its place. However, the replacement most always is deformed, often imitating a claw.

No matter the specific manifestation, and so long as the pedicles remain intact—the two permanent, hornlike skull pedestals from which annual antlers sprout—most injury-induced antler abnormalities are temporary, with subsequent racks reverting to normal. Contrarily, serious pedicle injuries, often resulting from rutting battles, can have a permanent and sometimes extreme influence on all future antlers, spawning drop-tines, massive clubs and other oddities in the extreme.

Additional common causes of antler abnormalities include malnutrition, testicular injury (leading to hormone imbalance) and trauma to other parts of the body, bones in particular, during antler growth.

Intriguingly, this latter phenomenon, known as "systemic influence," often leads to a deformed antler on the side opposite the injury. If, for example, a bull breaks his right rear leg in a fall (and survives), he may well produce a deformed left antler that year; somehow, the wiring gets crossed. While diseases, especially those caused by internal parasites, can also lead to systemic antler deformities, their effect is most often bilateral, distorting both antlers rather than just one.

And too, in the occasional gender confusion common to most all mammals (though never really common in any), you'll see the occasional antlerless bull or antlered cow; among wapiti (though not red deer), the latter more often than the former.

All apparent possibilities duly considered, it seems abundantly clear that this handsome fellow so happily harvesting dandelions just a rock's toss away is the product not of injury, disease or malnutrition, but of a genetic wild card.

Jokers wild.

And sadly, the joke's on him, in that natural selection in elk agrees with aesthetic preference among humans, strongly favoring antler symmetry. Even as female wapiti evidence a hankering for large, "balanced" antlers, they demonstrate an aversion to the bizarre. This, in turn, portends that the owners of perennially recurring nontypical racks will enjoy far fewer productive sexual encounters during their lives, prompting their quirky gene pools to dry up and blow away. Thus do the various cervids maintain millennial consistency in what has proven in each a functional antler form.

Yes, well, my fun can't last much longer. Even now, the bull raises his big bushy conk and glares suspiciously my way, perhaps having heard my booming heart, or caught a nervous tick of eyelid, or noted my out-of-place outline in his peripheral vision, or tasted on a shifty breeze a single terrifying molecule of man. Nor, I suppose, can we rule out the preternatural "sixth sense" that wild animals seem so often to possess.

I struggle to keep my cool, standing still as stone, and soon enough the giant deer relaxes and returns to murdering innocent sedge spears and wildflowers (if greens could scream, we'd have fewer self-righteous vegans in this bloody old world). But within moments and inevitably, a renegade zephyr queers the deal; the very instant I feel the breeze on the back of my neck, the bull barks like a foghorn and bounds away—vaulting easily over an obstacle-course of blowdown, dodging deftly among the tight upright tangle of trees, graceful as any steeple-chaser. For long lovely seconds after the animal has disappeared from sight, my ears continue to follow the cracking, popping, hoof-knocking trail of his panicked retreat.

At such times as this, I inevitably interrogate myself: Am I harassing wildlife by lurking almost daily through their turf? Certainly, when I get sloppy or the wind betrays or the forest spirits intervene and the animals find me out and flee with great to-do, I suppose "harassment" would seem to some a logical charge.

But then (he rationalizes), it's not as though this untrailed mountain, or any of the others I frequent, were overrun with hordes of humans hounding wildlife back and forth; I go most where others go least, and rarely the same place twice. And in winter, I carefully avoid going anywhere the wapiti may be, granting them the tranquillity they so desperately need when the snow is deep and the mercury low and good chow hard to find.

Moreover, with decades of practice under my belt (size 34 and holding), I don't really blow it all that often. And even when things do go wrong, I reason that things are still going right, convinced that by worming in amongst 'em and occasionally, inadvertently, prompting a brief panicked retreat, I'm helping wild wapiti to stay *wild* wapiti. After all, I could be a lurking cougar, a bad-ass bear or, as sometimes in fact I am, a hungry hunter.

Among the worst that can happen to wild animals, short-term and long, is for them to let their guard down, to relinquish their definitive caution and hair-trigger flight response. To do so, to become individually or generically relaxed, is to become easy prey or lowly semi-pets. This is my conviction.

And were I ever to abandon this primal game ... just look at all I'd miss! When I'm too old and moldy to do any better, then (perhaps) I'll warm a couch and watch the Discovery channel. But for now, for as far into the future as I can manage, I'll take my nature standing up.

Schlepping homeward, glowing inside and out under a pyrotechnic twilight, I reflect on my great good fortune, replaying and engraving the fantastical memories these rocky old mountains and this great green forest and that weirdly wondrous wapiti have given me this day—memories fit to last to the flickering final flame-out of my brief mortal tenure in this magnificent, ultimately unknowable heaven we call Earth.

Forgotten Elk
of the North

NOT LONG AGO, I was talking with Mike Mueller, a field director for the Rocky Mountain Elk Foundation, about the Foundation's recent rescue-purchase of a critical bit of wildlife habitat in North Dakota. The conversation soon enough got around to the elk that occupy that parcel—the least-known of North America's four living wapiti ecotypes—*Cervus elaphus manitobensis*.

We were mulling over the physical differences between the little-known Manitoban and the well-known Rocky Mountain, or Yellowstone regional variant, when Mike allowed as how "Manitoban elk are slightly bigger-bodied, and their pelage is a little darker."

"Seems that way," I acknowledged.

"And their antlers run a little smaller."

"So I hear tell."

"Even so," Mike went on, "most people looking at a group of Manitoban and Rocky Mountain bulls mixed together probably wouldn't be able to tell which from which."

"Don't know if *I* could," I admitted, having never met a *manitobensis* face to muzzle.

With these basics tacitly agreed upon, Mike upped the ante. "But when they bugle," he said, "it's easy to tell the difference between Canadian and below-the-border bulls."

This was a new one on me. Eager to learn more, I urged Mike to continue.

"Well," said he, "when a Rocky Mountain bull sings, it's *Aaaa-eeeee-aaaa ... a-unh, a-unh, a-unh*. But when a Canadian bull sounds off, it goes, *Aaaa-eeeee-aaaa ... eh?*"

Intrigued by our conversation, and not wanting to let ignorance make me the fall-guy for any more dumb jokes, I undertook forthwith to educate myself about the semi-anonymous cervid that *Bugle* editor Dan Crockett has dubbed "the forgotten elk of the north."

To prime the pump, I rounded up and perused all the literature on *C.e. manitobensis* I could find—disappointingly little, it turns out, and much of it less than fresh. Next, and for several days running, I used the telephone to bug wildlife managers, biologists and knowledgeable others from North Dakota to the Yukon, with frequent stops in between.

Only if you're interested, here's what I learned.

🌿

Current taxonomic consensus divides the North American wapiti, *Cervus elaphus*, into six "subspecies" (in fact and as we've seen, mere regional variants): Eastern, Merriam's, Manitoban, Rocky Mountain (Yellowstone), Roosevelt's (or Olympic, a native of the Pacific Northwest) and Tule (California). Sadly, the first two are—as mountain man Jim Bridger would have phrased it—gone beaver. And the third, the Manitoban, might as well be a ghost for all the attention it gets in the lower forty-eight.

In historic times, the Manitoban wapiti ranged across the southern half of its namesake province, west into southern and central Saskatchewan (with some spill-over into Alberta) and south into North Dakota and a tiny corner of Minnesota.

At the least.

I equivocate here because biologists Larry D. Bryant and Chris Maser, in their discussion of wapiti classification and distribution in *Elk of North America*, argue stridently that the Manitoban race, being prairie dwellers, likely occupied much of the prairie range that other scholars (specifically, Hall and Kelson in their prestigious *Mammals of North America*) have traditionally granted to the now-extinct Eastern elk.

If Bryant and Maser are correct, the Manitoban wapiti was once as much American as Canadian, ranging from central Canada as far south as the Red River along the Oklahoma-Texas border, and from the Front Range of the Rockies east to the Dakotas and south through Nebraska, Kansas and Oklahoma. The researchers base their hypothesis "on the evolution of natural habitats during and following the Wisconsin [most recent] glacial stage, and on the potential natural vegetation of North America [at that time]."

As I read it, Bryant and Maser are reasoning that since the Eastern elk evolved with and in the eastern deciduous forests, while the Manitoban elk evolved with and on the big bison grasslands of the Great Plains, it's logical to presume that the Eastern ecotype would have kept to the eastern forest ecology, to which it was adapted, while the Manitoban would have spread the length and breadth of the trans-border Great Plains, to which *it* was adapted.

Be all of that as it may (and I think it may), by early in the twentieth century, the Eastern elk had followed its Merriam's kin into the vast void of extinction. Meanwhile, the Manitoban race had been reduced to a precious few survivors holed up at Riding Mountain in southwestern Manitoba. In effect, Riding Mountain did for the Manitoban elk what Yellowstone National Park did for the Rocky Mountain elk, providing a last-minute, last-ditch bunker respite from extinction.

In the September, 1933, edition of *Canadian Field-Naturalist*, writer H. U. Green summarized the circumstances of the near-extinction and consequent hair's-breadth salvation of the Manitoban elk:

> The ease with which Wapiti could be destroyed individually and in numbers, and the value of their flesh to Indians and pioneer settlers, was in a great measure responsible for extravagant destruction. The creation of Riding Mountain as a Dominion Forest Reserve some 30 years ago alone saved what remained of the original herd by preserving a portion of their habitat, which otherwise would eventually have been tenanted by agriculturists.

Green went on to report that back in 1914, only "about 500 head of Wapiti ranged the Riding Mountains." By 1925 the number had risen to 2,000, while the 1933 population was "in the neighborhood of 3,500 head."

In the closing days of the twentieth century, the estimated elk population at Riding Mountain (a Canadian national park since 1930) is around five grand and growing—the largest herd of Manitoban wapiti extant. That figure was provided to me by Dr. Vince Crichton, provincial elk biologist for the Manitoba Wildlife Branch, and is based on an official, if by now somewhat antiquated, 1988 count.

In other parts of Manitoba (if you have one, you might want to glance at a Canadian map about now), the most recent (1988) elk demographics looked like this:

Duck Mountain Provincial Park—1,500
Porcupine Provincial Forest—300
Spruce Woods Provincial Forest and Park—500
Interlake (the region between Lakes Manitoba and Winnipeg):
    North—100; South—200
Miscellaneous—500

That ciphers out to some 8,400 wapiti for the entirety of Manitoba, less or more. Likely more: According to provincial elk biologist Peter Hildebrand, a more sophisticated and accurate count, based on satellite technology, was conducted at Duck Mountain in January of 1993. This aerial census actually *saw* more than 1,450 elk, suggesting a population as high as two thousand.

Since a population-reduction hunt had been conducted during the three-year period 1989–91 in response to elk-caused damage to agricultural lands bordering the Duck Mountain preserve, removing some twelve hundred wapiti from the herd, the 1988 count obviously was low: You don't kill all but three hundred members of an isolated elk population, then just a couple of years later have two thousand. Hildebrand believes the actual 1988 Duck Mountain population was perhaps 2,200 to 2,500 animals.

Generalizing outward from Duck Mountain (something Hildebrand, being a good scientist, was reluctant to do, but which I, a mere backwoods scrivener, have no problem with), it seems possible that elk populations in Manitoba's other preserves were also under-counted in '88, giving the province considerably more elk today than the advertised 8,400.

But no one knows for sure. Nor, I guess, do precise stats matter all that much. What does matter is that the wildlife managers and biologists I spoke with, along with RMEF Canadian field rep Lyle Dorey, agree that Manitoba's elk are holding their own, or better, in most areas.

As it is down here in the States, hunting is a necessary and efficient management tool for Canadian elk. While only an average of two to four hundred wapiti are taken by licensed hunters in Manitoba each year, an unknown but significant additional number are killed by poachers and First Nation peoples (the Canadian PC term for Indians), driving the total annual kill up to ... who knows?

"If I had to guess," offers Crichton, "I'd guess that natives take more elk than do licensed hunters."

In all my talks with Canadian biologists and wildlife managers, I sensed a deep distrust of the efficacy of current native hunting privileges. While Indians must follow pretty much the same rules as other Canadians regarding where they can hunt (Riding Mountain and other preserves are off-limits to everyone, and permission must be gained to hunt on private lands), Canadian Indians are not required to purchase licenses, they may hunt year-round and at night (spotlighting along logging roads is a popular "traditional" activity), they may take both antlered and antlerless animals and they needn't report their kills.

This Big Unknown is a monumental management migraine for Canadian wildlife officials, though few are willing to complain about it, at least not on the record, for exactly the same career-fear reasons U.S. bureaucrats too often withhold their true thoughts. Near as I can ferret it out, only one scientific inquiry has been made regarding this troublesome and touchy situation. In a 1989 master's thesis, Kenneth Rebizant—now a biologist with the Manitoba Wildlife Branch—studied the survival rates of male *C. e. manitobensis* (known to be low) at Spruce Woods Provincial Park and environs. From Rebizant's abstract:

> The causes of the low male to antlerless elk ratios observed during winter aerial surveys ... were investigated. ... The survivorship of radio-transmittered males was low. ... The low numbers of male elk in the Spruce Woods population was attributed to differential natural mortality, dispersal of immature males from the population and male bias in poaching and Indian harvests.

Rebizant's study, while stopping short of suggesting conscious abuse by native hunters, nonetheless highlights one of the deepest pitfalls of unmanaged hunting: Too many bulls can and probably will be taken from a herd, leading to a dangerously low bull-to-cow ratio—dangerous because it adversely affects breeding success, breeding timing and, consequently, calf survivability. Cows bred late give late birth to their calves, who in turn have less time to gain critical weight before the onset of the first killing, culling winter. And Manitoban wildlife managers are helpless to deal with it.

Yet, as Dr. Crichton notes (perhaps in hopes of fostering a self-fulfilling prophesy?), "many of our native peoples are coming to recognize the need to work with the rest of society if they want to continue to enjoy the hunting privileges that traditionally have been afforded them."

While I empathize, intellectually and to varying degrees, with both sides, my heart is with the wapiti.

Moving west into Saskatchewan, I tracked down provincial elk specialist Ed Kowal—on vacation, at home on a Sunday afternoon. Even so, Kowal indulged my litany of ignorant questions and we talked elk for a good long while.

Unlike Manitoba, where the majority of wapiti are ganged up on a handful of preserves and can be hunted only when they wander down and out onto Crown and private lands in winter, the majority of Saskatchewan's eight thousand or so Manitoban elk range through large expanses of non-preserve public lands. A sampling:

• On its eastern border, the province shares Duck Mountain Park with Manitoba, with perhaps two hundred elk living on the Saskatchewan side.

• The northern provincial forests region, northeast of Hudson Bay, hosts the bulk of Saskatchewan's Manitobans. There, elk roam through a heavily logged (and, consequently, heavily roaded, hunted and poached), mixed-age aspen forest ecology.

• The northernmost elk pocket in Saskatchewan, lying along the east side of the province, is the Cumberland Delta, a good stretch above Hudson Bay, which hosts some four hundred wapiti. A recent "bit of a decline" in the population there has prompted wildlife managers to suspect modest predation by timber wolves. (And if so—why not? Wolves are native subsistence hunters too.)

• Over on the western border, a herd of four to five hundred Manitobans haunts the Fort A La Corne Provincial Forest.

• Meanwhile, down in the southwest corner of the province, some fourteen hundred Manitobans roam the Cypress Hills Provincial Park region.

Saskatchewan, like Manitoba, also has problems with poaching and unregulated native hunting. But blessed with a more manageable management situation, Saskatchewan has been able to do something about it.

"Most unregulated elk hunting," Ed Kowal explains, "takes place in the northern provincial forests—all those logging roads. Consequently, back in 1983 we embarked on a road-closure program and created a lot of road-corridor game preserves as well. With the road closures and preserves, we've been able to rebuild big game populations which, previous to 1983, were falling off the face of the earth. Moose increased 60 percent in just two years. Elk numbers aren't as well documented, but they have definitely benefited as well."

Additionally, transplant programs, especially in the west of the province, are being undertaken to help increase and broaden Saskatchewan's elk population.

Finally and farther west yet, out in Alberta, a hefty herd of Manitobans enjoys total protection at aptly named Elk Island National Park. Due to the park's modest size and burgeoning populations of wapiti, bison and other wildlife, it's become possible, even necessary, to trap and relocate some three hundred elk each year—a boon to other regions.

Map check: Back-stroking east, to southern Manitoba's Spruce Woods Provincial Forest, then angling southeast along the Pembina River, across the international border and down into North Dakota, we encounter a most interesting "semi-native" Manitoban elk herd—the herd Mike Mueller and I had discussed.

While both *Mammals of North America* and *Elk of North America* agree that northern North Dakota was within the historic range of the Manitoban wapiti ecotype, all the elk on the American side were either killed or driven back north across the border during pioneer settlement of the area. Since that time, North Dakota was without a viable Manitoban elk population.

Then, sometime during the late 1970s or early '80s, a small herd of Canadian wapiti repatriated the state on their own.

At least, it's *presumed* they're Manitobans. Big game biologist Roger Johnson of North Dakota Game and Fish, playing the devil's advocate, points out that no efforts have been undertaken to *prove* the new arrivals are Canucks. Even so, most authorities agree it's much more than likely that the immigrants are in fact Manitobans. And in their southward migration, they probably followed the selfsame route we just traced on the map—from Manitoba's Spruce Woods Provincial Forest (the most proximate source), down through the Pembina River Valley (a natural wildlife corridor), then south and east across the U.S. border to their new-old North Dakota home.

Johnson concurs with this scenario, pointing out that shortly before the first elk showed up in North Dakota, Manitoba had held a special hunt in the Spruce Woods area, purposely and forcibly dispersing its elk. "That hunt," Johnson says, "is likely the reason we have elk down here today."

The habitat the invaders have occupied is a mixture of private agricultural and state wildlife lands in and along the Pembina and Tongue river valleys.

"It's rugged, beautiful country," says Mike Mueller. "You're driving through boring grain fields, then all of a sudden you drop down into the big gorgeous valleys of the Pembina and Tongue rivers, their waters draining off toward Canada. Locals call it 'the bush.' It's good, thick wildlife cover—a mix of aspen and hardwoods with a rich understory. Not only elk, but Canadian moose, white-tailed deer, black bears, ruffed grouse and even an occasional wolf shelter in there. And directly above the gorges is all that yummy agricultural land, with fingers of bushy cover poking out into it."

By the mid-1980s, North Dakota's Pembina herd had grown large enough to support (or require, depending on your view) limited hunting. Ron Stromstad, chief of the wildlife division for North Dakota Game and Fish, says that today the herd comprises 100 to 150 animals—a population sufficient to prompt a ten-tag annual draw hunt for residents. Hunter success averages an impressive 65 percent.

Hunter support—moral, political and especially financial—for this burgeoning local elk population has been enthusiastic and generous. Nor does that come as a surprise—hunters, after all, historically have provided a whopping 80 percent of the funding for all wildlife programs in America. (While, to my knowledge, no hard-core "animal welfare" group has ever given one thin dime to benefit wildlife or wildlife habitat.)

What does come as a bit of a surprise is that local landowner support is also sky-high. After all, the Pembina elk, being elk, occasionally raid area farms and ranches, gobbling and trampling crops and committing other economic improprieties that agriculturalists generally loathe. But elk are such a novelty up that way, most affected landowners feel the show is worth its admission price.

Additionally, the crucial two-hundred acre parcel recently purchased by the Rocky Mountain Elk Foundation helps to sew together a patchwork of Pembina Gorge wildlife habitat and protect it permanently from development.

🍃

By way of concluding my Canadian wapiti research binge, I circled back to the beginning to reflect briefly on the "common-knowledge" truths about Manitoban elk that Mike Mueller and I had so blithely agreed upon: specifically, that Manitobans have darker coloring, larger bodies and smaller antlers than their stateside brethren.

The easiest first: The darker coloring of Manitoban elk is subtle, but visually verifiable, particularly in summer.

Concerning the size of Manitoban elk—it's a matter of record. Former Manitoba provincial elk specialist Duane Davies, as well as Vince Crichton and other authorities, report that Manitoban bulls weighing in the vicinity of eleven hundred pounds show up too often to be anomalies. The only other wapiti population to equal or exceed the Manitoban's weight records is a small group of Olympic elk transplanted some years ago to Afognak Island, Alaska. Your legendary half-ton Rocky Mountain bull, meanwhile, is rare as an ecologically altruistic land developer.

Another accepted biological index of relative size between subspecies is skull volume—and a pair of Manitoban elk skulls from Riding Mountain are the largest known to exist.

Bigger skulls, you'd think, would sprout bigger antlers. But a search of the Boone & Crockett Club's *Records of North American Big Game* doesn't show many Manitobans near the top. In fact, it doesn't show any Manitobans anywhere, per se, since the tallies aren't broken down by "subspecies." The best a curious person can do is to assume that antlers listed as originating in Manitoba and Saskatchewan were produced by Manitoban elk.

Looking for clarification, I consulted Vince Crichton, a member of the Manitoba Big Game Trophy Association involved in putting together the group's 1992 record book. The *current* number one Manitoban typicals, Crichton reports (an even larger rack exists, but has not yet been officially entered), was killed at Duck Mountain in 1978. It scored 413⁴/₈ B&C points.

Granted, the world record wapiti—an infamous Colorado bull killed by a meat-hunting miner back in 1899—goes 442³/₈. Still, 413⁴/₈ is hardly *little*.

(Note: These "scores" equate to the total inches reckoned through a convoluted system of measurements, including length and circumference of main beams, total tine length and the widest distance, or "spread," between main beams. Symmetry is rewarded by deducting any difference between the two sides from the total score. On the one hand, score-keeping for purposes of ranking "trophies" is a silly little game for silly little boys and girls with deep insecurities manifested through outsized egos. On the other hand, the "books" provide a useful statistical warehouse for cervid scientists, wildlife managers and those, like me, who are merely interested.)

Moreover, when we shift the focus from typical antlers to nontypicals, we come hard against a gargantuan 447¹/₈ Manitoban rack that ranks ... number one in the world.

The story of Canadian hunter Jim Berry and his world-record nontypical elk, taken during the winter of 1961 north of Riding Mountain, is reminiscent of turn-of-the-century Colorado hunter John Plute and his long-standing world-record typical: Like Plute, Berry was out for meat, not antlers. And like Plute, Berry bothered to lug the cumbersome rack home only because of its exceptional grandeur. After all, the Canadian hunter had some 560 pounds of meat to deal with, carved from an animal estimated to have weighed more than twelve hundred pounds on the hoof.

The Berry rack weighs thirty-eight pounds, carries eight points on the right beam, nine on the left, with fifty-one inch mains and a fifty-four inch spread. It's in the spread, primarily, that Manitobans lose out to their Yellowstone kin. Beams and tines also seem to run a bit shorter on the average. But Manitoban racks tend to be extraordinarily beefy. Duane Davies has collected data confirming this contention. And Vince Crichton, who towers six-foot-six plus some, says he's examined several Manitoban racks so massive he couldn't get a hand around the bases of the main beams.

In sum, Manitoban elk antlers do, on the average, run some smaller than those of Yellowstone elk, but still can be astoundingly huge, and are beautiful in any event.

Although there aren't all that many Manitobans up there— probably fewer than twenty thousand in all of Canada, with North Dakota and Minnesota tossed in for good measure—the no-longer forgotten elk of the north don't have to sing second bugle to any wapiti anywhere in terms of their handsomeness, the rugged beauty of their home or the wildness and majesty with which they invest both the landscape and the hearts of those who know them.

Alone in the Dark

Through the Jungle very softly flits a shadow and a sigh—He is
Fear, O Little Hunter, he is Fear!—Kipling

A COUPLE OF HOURS before dark, the clarion silence of the aspen grove is interrupted by a muffled snap of limb, like an elk padding around in house slippers. A moment later, a chimera of brown floats like a dream through the trees beyond the spring pool I'm watching from an impromptu ground blind (a stump to sit on and a screen of brush behind). As always at times like this, my heart hits passing gear.

When the animal steps into the open a few seconds later, the adrenaline rush almost knocks me off my log: This is no wild-flower-nibbling wapiti, but the biggest black bear of the nine I've seen so far this year. The bruin is only thirty yards out and in-bound fast, almost as if he's spotted me and doesn't like what he sees.

Which is not to say the bear is "charging," which he, or she, is not, and which black bears rarely do (notwithstanding some nitwit New York editor once shoved such greenhorn inanity into my mouth, so to speak). Still, any way you cut it, there's a real big bear headed my way and I suddenly feel distinctly small.

Thinking *Hugh Glass redux* (already an old favorite exit fantasy of mine years before it was co-opted for the hokey Bart the Bear climax in the film version of Jim Harrison's classic *Legends of the Fall* ... but all of that can wait), I long for the hunting knife buried beyond reach in the bottom of my day pack. Likewise, I crave the canister of pepper spray I wear holstered quick-draw at my belt in grizzly country, but rarely bother with here in civilized SoCal-orado.

Twenty yards ... fifteen ... on comes the bear, not running, not charging, yet closing with seeming intent. Lacking any brighter idea, or any idea at all, I just sit and stare. When the big brown blackie gets to ten yards, I suppose I'll jump up and shout "Boo!"

But at a dozen paces the bear suddenly stops, lifts his black-nosed brown muzzle to sample the evening breeze, cocks his bucket-big head and peers uphill, intrigued by something invisible to my humble human senses—then goes shambling off toward ... whatever. Gone with the wind.

In instant-replay retrospect, relaxing, I seriously doubt that the bear ever knew I was here; and he/she/it certainly wasn't "coming for me." Even grizzlies rarely attack humans unprovoked, and black bears almost never. More likely, I just happened to be sitting, camouflaged and anonymous, where he just happened to be headed. Such accidental close encounters are among the many wild and wonderful roadside attractions attendant to hard-core, out-and-amongst-'em wildlife watching.

My pulse has barely idled down from the bear encounter when a distant bugle animates the autumn forest. Across the next half hour, the proclamation is repeated at roughly ten-minute intervals, sounding each time from a little closer. Gradually, my initial elation turns to despair; a pattern is emerging here that isn't in the least reassuring for my purposes. From the sounds of it, the bull is contouring across a heavily wooded slope a couple hundred yards above me, headed, most likely, for Cow Spring, another pool along this extended aspen bench that comprises the heart of my personal wapiti world. Ironically, it was Cow Spring where I sat last evening, to absolutely no avail.

I consider trying to bend the bull my way with a challenging bugle or a coy cow chirp—then reflect on the number of times calling has backfired with these savvy suburban elk. Nor can I risk a stalk, what with the fall forest floor a litter of crispy leaves and the breeze untenable and my quarry on the move. Stuck with the status quo, at least for now, I settle in to enjoy the concert—which, in itself, is reason enough to be here.

Following an intermission of several minutes, the bugling resumes with redoubled verve, ringing once from the vicinity of Cow Spring, again from a hundred yards below. Oddly, the bull seems to be jogging back and forth along the length of the spring seep, bugling first from the top, then from the bottom. Odder yet, each time he bugles from the lower position, he sounds somehow different; smaller, maybe. After several minutes of this, it finally sinks in that I'm hearing not one, but two bulls.

Soon a third, distinctly foreign voice joins the wapiti. It's a raven, circling low between Cow Spring and me, blue-black wings gleaming in the soft September sun, croaking out a raspy chant that sounds—I kid thee not—like *Elk! Elk!*

On impulse, ignoring my own best advice, I opt to try and bugle the buglers in. Even should they shut up and slip away, as so often they are wont to do, they won't have seen or scented me, and I'll have achieved my primary goal of subtly intruding into their domain, enjoying some sort of intimate, animate contact with them—watching, hearing, even just smelling—then sneaking back out, all without the wapiti (and, in this case, one bear) ever knowing I was around.

My initial bugle—imperfect but passable—is answered with resounding silence. Nonetheless, having committed myself, I blow a second chorus and am more than a little surprised when the bigger-sounding of the two bulls not only answers, but stokes the fire with a five-note postscript chuckle. For the next half hour, the big bull and I have a grand old time swapping insults. The smaller bull, meanwhile, has butted out, gone silent.

Predictably, the battle of the bugles soon degenerates to a stand-off; my boisterous opponent is all blow and no show. I'm thinking about trying to sneak in close enough for a peek—the distance between us is only a couple hundred yards—when a twig snaps close beside me. I crank only my eyeballs around and catch a dark form slipping through the trees near where the bear first appeared not so long ago. Has he circled around for another go? Trying to put a sneak on me?

Half an anxious minute passes before a long-legged 5x5 appears and comes tip-toeing down the hill toward me. The cloven-hooved beast, fresh from a wallow and coated with dark-chocolate mud, shines black as any moose and smells like trouble. On he comes, circling around the spring pool and stopping just on the far side of the same bushy little spruce I'm snuggled into for cover. From he to me is but five yards ... and there he makes his stand: ears erect, red eyes roving, nostrils flared. Only catatonia, camouflage, a benevolent breeze and some seriously dumb luck preserve my anonymity.

Meanwhile, from over at Cow Spring, the bullish cursing continues. It's tempting to deduce that these two fellows have conspired to work together, the bigger bull keeping me bugling and distracted while his apprentice slips in to reconnoiter the situation. Old-school wildlife biologists detest anthropomorphism, but as a mere humble hunter, woodsman and watcher, I am free to believe my own senses. And I do sense and believe that animals, wild animals at least (a major goal of domestication is dumbing animals down), know a heck of a lot more than we give them credit for. And at the moment, it occurs to me that there's a wapiti conspiracy going down.

For long electric minutes (three or four, maybe; an eternity in such stressful circumstances) the bull just stands there, a still-life of himself, as I kneel, barely breathing, trembling with animal delight.

Unwelcome relief comes with the next pronouncement from Cow Spring. Apparently hearing some subtle message in the senior bull's bugle that's wasted on me, the scout bull grunts—not an alarm bark; just a mildly disgusted *"Huh!"*—then turns and strides away. A few seconds more, and the five-by disappears into the brush and blowdown, probably gone to report to the boss.

Silence. Darkness.

Come morning, I'm back on the mountain before sunrise, squatting on a timbered ledge above the still-dark aspen bench. With the first glow of dawn I ease down the slope to a wide spot on a game trail just above Cow Spring. This is one of my favorite elk-watching haunts, in that it offers excellent visibility, favorable wind currents, good hiding cover and high elk traffic, with spectacular scenery to boot. I settle in for the wait.

Across the next couple of hours, birds flock to the pool to drink and splash, chirping gaily. Squirrels gambol and chatter. A hungry-eyed pine marten passes in ghostly silence, bringing an abrupt end to the squirrels' careless merriment. The air warms, flies buzz and my eyelids begin to sag. Midmorning, one lazy bugle echoes down from someplace up the mountain. Nap time.

More time passes and I'm about to grab a nap my ownself when I'm startled to alertness by the nearby croaking, like a goose with laryngitis, of a raven. Another raven, that is. Judging by its raspier voice, this is not the same bird as last evening. And rather than *Elk! Elk!*, this overgrown old crow seems to be yelling *Look! Look!* I turn and peer in the direction of the calls and, sure enough, back in the dark tangle of spruce and fir directly below the circling bird I see the graceful pistoning movements of four long, slender legs. Coyote ... no, a mule deer doe. Small, sleek and alone. A yearling.

Without hesitation or sound the doe glides to the spring, lowers her long lovely neck and drinks. I stifle a toothy smile for fear she might see. Soon sated, the doe departs none the wiser and stasis returns to the forest, a peaceful silence interrupted only by the restful twittering of restless birds and occasional breezy gossip among the brittle aspens.

It's evening before the next round of excitement begins, its approach heralded by a close, distinct *Crack!* of heavy hoof treading on a dry fallen limb. And another. No house slippers this time.

Within minutes the noisemakers appear—a roan-dark cow trailed close at heel by a long-limbed calf. The cow is clearly nervous, though I can't figure why. The evening breeze is soft and steady and running downhill from she to me. And, as always, I'm fully camouflaged, including gloves and a face-net. I did not walk through where the elk now stand, nor have I made a sound or twitched a finger all evening. Even so, the cow approaches the spring with obvious tredpidation, stopping frequently to stare in my direction. I respond by squinting my eyes, hiding their whites to mute the sixth-sense "feel" of a dead-on stare. Perhaps (my best guess), these are local animals who have visited this place often enough to have memorized the vegetation patterns and recognize that I don't belong. Or maybe it's just a mother's protective instincts.

In any event, thirst eventually overcomes caution. The cow moves gingerly to the spring, wades in and lowers her huge coffin-shaped head to drink. I can clearly hear the sucking sounds as she vacuums water in, horselike, through clenched teeth, her Adam's apple running up and down, up and down, busy as an oasis well-bucket. Still nervous, every few seconds the cow snaps her head up and peers about, diamonds of water dribbling from her chin. After this unhurried fashion, several minutes pass while she sates her long deep thirst.

Finally done, Cautious Cow shoots me a farewell glare and stomps away. Her calf follows without drinking. Their heavy, careless steps fade gradually into the forest silence and I am left alone with my thoughts ... of which, I suppose, I have entirely too many. Especially as dark approaches.

Time passes, as time is wont to do.

It's tempting at this juncture to trot out the trusty old crepuscular cliché, *the evening shadows grew long.* But the growing is history now; my whole world is shadow—that ethereal twilight zone when our deepest and most ancient dread comes out to play with our minds. I'm speaking, of course, of the visceral fear of being caught out deep in the woods ... alone, in the dark.

From ghoulies and ghosties and long-leggety beasties And things that go bump in the night, Good Lord, deliver us! (traditional Cornish prayer).

To the man who is afraid, everything rustles (Sophocles).

In many ways it's perfectly practical—this universal human unease with the unseen, the unknown and the unknowable, with things that go bump and rustle in the night—having been imprinted in human instinct through thousands of ancestral generations, a million years of nights spent huddled close in the flickering security of quivering caves of firelight, peering blindly, anxiously into the hungry void ... listening, listening.

Yet, in my case at least, it's not the anthracite night, per se, that makes me squirm and fidget nearly so much as its precursor ... that twilight crack in the universe when the impossible seems all too likely and the urge to scurry back to the security of home and hearth, or at least to camp and campfire—to get home *before* dark—can at times be overpowering.

Trouble is, as a serious wildlife watcher (a term I prefer to "amateur naturalist"), the evening twilight is often the most lucrative few minutes of the entire day, a magical moment pregnant with possibility.

In struggling to maintain my macho self-image as a recovering Marine and veteran woodsman, I try to rationalize this recurring twilight timidity with tricks of logic, to wit: Caroline will be worried if I'm not home soon after dark; Caroline will not be pleased if she has to hold dinner too late; walking out in the dark portends a heightened clumsiness, assuring more racket and a bolder scent trail due to increased contact with foliage, both of which work to defeat my best attempts not to let wildlife know I've come and gone. And so on.

And it's true: Such nocturnal complications provide *logical* reasons aplenty to relinquish the day a few minutes early and get the hell out of Dodge while the gettin's good.

But alas, it's not a logic thing. It's a visceral thing, an evolutionary memory from an infinitely wilder past, and any outdoorsman (or woman) who denies ever having felt uneasy as darkness engulfed him (or her) in some remote and unfamiliar place, far from home or camp, is pulling his (or her) own leg. But not mine.

Rather than try to deny my nocturnal willies, I've learned to deal with them by coaching myself to stay put "just one more minute," one slow minute at a time, staring hard into the gathering gloom, searching for the slightest shadow of movement and ... listening.

Always listening.

In fact, it's in largest part a listening thing, this deep-woods evening wapiti watching. Occasionally you'll see elk coming, sure. And if the wind is right, the trained nose can sound the alarm (so to speak), at least for rutting bulls. (Oh how I love that pungent, lusty stench!) Yet for the most part, it's a listening thing. Listening and learning.

Learning to identify the sharp, arboreal snap of a brittle branch breaking under the hurled weight of a squirrel ... coming to know the bafflingly big sounds made by that same rowdy rodent scurrying through sere autumn leaves ... growing accustomed to the distracting *chuck-chuck-chuck* of sap-heavy spruce cones clunking down through tangled limbs before thudding to earth like dud hand grenades ... and, through the process of learning to "weigh" forest noises, ultimately reaching a place where, far more often than not, you can distinguish each of these very similar sounds, and a great many others, from the heavy hollow knock of elk hoof striking blowdown.

Withal, it's called woodcraft. It's the product of ongoing curiosity and careful attention to detail. It once meant survival, it doubtless contributed to the development of intelligence as we know it and, sadly, in these hurried, gadget-ridden, shallow, short-cutting times as we approach a self-afflicted global apocalypse, it's an art, and a pleasure, all but lost. Listening, that is.

Light thickens, the crow Makes wing to the rooky wood; Good things of day begin to droop and drowse, Whiles night's black agents to their preys do rouse. (Macbeth)

The squirrels and birds suddenly go quiet, and an eerie stillness consumes all. It's now or never; soon or not tonight. I redouble my attention, forcing my humble senses deep into the silent shadows below me, scanning for any hint of anything animate, struggling to ignore my growing unease with the growing darkness.

In the passage from day to night there is to me always something mysterious. In the forest that hour is mournful and sad. Around reigns an oppressive silence. Then the ear just catches some barely audible sound, as though a distant sigh. Whence does it come? (V. K. Arseniev)

In my case, in this case, it comes from behind, jerking me unceremoniously out of my tranced musings—my name, whispered. The voice is young and soft, hauntingly familiar yet just beyond recognition's reach, filling me instantly with a bittersweet sense of love and loss. I whirl around and peer intently into the gloom, staring as if into the past ... but no one and nothing is there. Just some lonely evening breeze, I suppose, sighing through the trees.

The experience leaves me shaken, unsteady, alone. Can't say why, there seems no connection, but suddenly I think of the big brown black bear, so recently so close. *Still* close, out there somewhere even now.

Hang on, man. Hang in. One more minute (I tell myself, one slow minute at a time) and you're *outta here*. Elk or no elk. Another day of this precious life gone, forever and forever.

Carpe diem advises Horace, that smug old sage. But as so often happens when out in nature, the day has seized *me*; I want it never to end. Even this, even now. Especially this and now.

Yet insidiously, inevitably, irrevocably, immutably, implacably, it does end. Camera light is long since gone and seeing light is waning fast, at least down here on this gloomy timbered bench. Night has come, and the elk have not. No more bears, neither.

Silently as possible I repack my pack, hang pack on back, stand, stretch, tip-toe up the near-vertical east-facing slope that shelters and defines this cloistered woodsy pocket, topping out winded on a rocky ledge where twilight yet lingers, if only just barely.

And here I stop to blow. As my heartbeat quiets and the silence flows back in like displaced water, I hear it, ringing loud as laughter from the jet black unknown below ... *Crack!* A few moments pass in utter silence ... *Crack!* Onward it comes, bumping and rustling ever closer, approaching the very spring pool I've just spent five hours watching.

Splash!

Ain't it the way?

Well, tomorrow's another day, at least if we're lucky. With the revealing light of sunrise I'll return to this ridge, to the aspen bench below, transformed by old friend Sol from black and foreboding to bright and green and friendly—to inspect the big split prints I know will pock the mud around the spring pool (hell, they're being made even now), to sniff the fresh-scuffed earth for tell-tale pheromones (bull or cow?), to resume the thrilling wait.

Until then, for now, I turn and melt into the night—alone in the dark.

When Elk Get
in Their Licks

ON WHAT BEGAN as a fine summer's day, a game warden friend and I marched mule-back up a local mountain (just one among many) to see what we could see. In addition to exercising Kevin's mules and getting some good high fresh air, we both were curious about how the habitat and wildlife were faring up there, following two consecutive summers of heavy cattle grazing.

As I'd feared, the flowery parks and grassy hillsides, where prior to the grazing I'd roamed happily among elk, deer and bear, had been reduced to thistle, other noxious non-native weeds and cow pies. The banks of what had been a drinking-pure spring creek—many's the time in years past I've knelt there beside fresh elk tracks to guzzle directly from the sparkling rill—were trampled and eroded, the water muddy and dung-fouled, the trout all gone. Oh well, it's private land, fair game for abuse by our cultural code.

Anxious to escape this "wise use" disaster area, we fled on up the mountain as fast as our mulish plugs would condescend to plod. In due time we crossed an invisible, unfenced boundary separating private land from national forest (more than a few loose-boweled bovines obviously had done likewise), eventually climbing far enough above the creek to escape the mess. To the stockman's credit, he had at least put out salt blocks in an attempt to hold his beeves on the private land he was leasing, and in fact most of the animals were obediently wadded up creekside. But salt is no substitute for manageable, ecologically conscionable herd sizes and responsible cowboying. And such ganging along riparian corridors is hard as hell on habitat.

Another hour and we were into fresh territory, well above where all my previous, leg-powered solo outings had been terminated by fatigue or darkness.

At the crest of a broad bench, the fragrant ponderosa forest we'd been riding through opened into a long, slender, grassy park along whose sunken belly trickled a silvery spring seep, dotted here and there with the muddy, piss-smelling wallows of rutting bull elk. But happily, nary a moo-poo in sight. We urged our sturdy steeds, Red and Freckles, on up through the kidney-shaped clearing and into a flicker-shaded, spice-smelling, summer-green grove of quaking aspens.

It was in amongst the quakies that we found it: a huge old fir stump squatting there, hoary with age, two muscular surface roots reaching out like big open arms. And cradled between those arms was a revelation. The earth at the base of the stump, between the two outstretched roots, had been excavated, pawed-out in fact, leaving a washtub-sized crater of fulvous mud. And trampled into that mud was a wafflework of elk and deer prints.

I glanced at Kevin, and he—having a master's degree in zoology and a decade of experience as a professional wildlife manager—nodded and said simply, "Lick."

Of course! I felt dumb, *was* dumb, for not having immediately recognized it as such myself; I'd been thinking wallow, not really thinking at all. Dismounting and wandering about, we found an intricate network of game trails, deep-trod and active, leading to the lick like spokes to a hub. I'm a naturally curious sort, and the temptation was to confirm my friend's salty opinion by sampling a finger of mud from the pit. But the lick was obviously a lick and pretty darn funky, so I let pseudo-science slide.

Exciting as hell (somewhat more than, no doubt) to discover such a place as this—another hidden secret of the mountain forests revealed, another warm green summer memory to carry me through the weary, monochromatic months of winter pending. This lick, I reflected—if not discovered and destroyed by beef cows or domestic sheep or bulldozed over by road-building loggers—this lick will continue to add spice to the lives of wild creatures (including the very few adventurous humans ever likely to stumble across it) far beyond my puny lifetime. Such knowledge, such edgy trust, is reassuring—granting us what my old Montana friend Bud Guthrie liked to call "a piece of everlasting."

Having miles yet to go and with the afternoon running low, and after a good long look, we reluctantly left the lick behind and rode off through the aspens ... and within a hundred yards flushed a big wad of wapiti bedded in a deep pool of shade; they must have taken our mounts' thudding hoof-falls for their own kind, to have let us get so close.

When the elk had gone (didn't take long), we rode over to where they'd been and dismounted to check out their nests (elk-hearts always do that kind of stuff). Judging it to be a most pleasant place, we plopped right down to munch our lunches. A few minutes later, when I wished aloud as how I'd brought some salt for my cold-turkey sandwich, my wise-acre buddy reminded me of the briny lick-mud just down the way, suggesting, "Bet it spreads like peanut butter."

In silent response, I moved upwind of Kevin and lit a cigar.

Clouds had been gathering for hours, a fresh breeze had risen and, just as we were preparing to move along, a bolt of lightning—as unexpected as a bolt of lightning—lashed out from the troubled heavens and struck far too close, heralding a schizophrenic electrical storm that came double-timing in, hazing us into our slickers for a jolting jenny race back down the mountain, shouting as we went—like Monty Python's courageous knights in *Search for the Holy Grail*— "Run away!"

Such memories, the bad with the good, are the salt of an out-doors life.

🌿

While variety may well be the spice of our intellectual and love lives, the spice of biological life is salt. Not merely a pleasing food additive, salt is a life-essential nutrient.

Life, after all, began in the seas, and sea water remains the ar-chetypal saline solution, with salt comprising some two-thirds of all dissolved solids suspended therein. So deep are our evolu-tionary roots sunk in saltwater that the very blood piping through our veins mimics it.

A primary task salt performs in the body is the regulation of osmotic pressure, or the level of water retention. Salt is also es-sential to the efficient transmission of nerve impulses. Moreover, a critical ingredient in the stomach's digestive juices is hydro-chloric acid—the "chloric" portion closely bound with salt. We—and wapiti, and all other mammals for that matter—quite simply can't live without salt, though the amounts required are minimal and generally available in that elusive "balanced diet" we hear so much about but so rarely suffer ourselves to follow.

On the other foot, for an unfortunate minority of folks, any-thing more than a very little salt—as we're cautioned *ad nau-seam* by the health police—can lead to a condition of excess fluid retention called edema, a troublesome contributor to hyperten-sion, better known as "high blood pressure."

Even so, and notwithstanding its moderate potential dangers, so essential and *desirable* is salt to humans that it has been an im-portant trade item—on occasion even used as currency—throughout recorded history. Salt has even sneaked its way into modern language in various offshoots of its original meaning: The English "salary," for a lucrative example, descends from the Latin *salarium*, a cash allowance paid to Roman soldiers for the purchase of salt.

Common table salt—sodium chloride (NaCl)—is a natural element found not only suspended in sea water, but in solid land deposits as the mineral halite, appearing variously as grains, crystals and compact masses. Some halite deposits are thousands of feet thick and malleable enough to bend to geophysical pressures and dome up like subterranean volcanoes, warping the earth above and around them. Salt domes, in fact, were major players in sculpting the moonscape geology of southeastern Utah, at Arches National Park and elsewhere. And, of course, anyplace a finger of salt pokes through to the surface, elk, mountain goats, bighorn sheep and other wild ungulates aren't long in finding it.

Livestock, too, like to get in their licks—a fact long recognized by stockmen, who, like bartenders putting out free pretzels, use salt to bribe their customers into staying put in certain areas, most often near water, thereby gaining at least a modicum of control over where the moronic mooers and brainless bleaters roam, and where they don't. And for the rancher willing to pay a very little extra, salt blocks with trace minerals blended in are available, mimicking naturally occurring deposits and providing multiple health advantages at a single lick.

Considering all of this—that salt is essential to the lives and health of all mammals, that ungulates crave salt, that elk and other wildlife eagerly utilize natural mineral licks and that salt blocks have proven to be at least a modestly effective tool for the manipulation of livestock movements across open range—wildlife managers long ago began pondering the question: Can salt be successfully employed to influence the seasonal distribution of big game animals? If so, the common, economical salt block's uses as a wildlife management tool would be manifold.

The earliest and to date still the only extensive studies along these lines were conducted on the Nez Perce National Forest in Idaho, beginning in 1921 and continuing sporadically through 1960. The banner study year was 1947, when 235 *tons* of block salt came hurtling from the sky like God's own hailstorm.

And what were the results of this extensive, expensive testing— other, perhaps, than to end the careers of any unfortunate creatures upon whose heads the eighty-pound bombs might have landed?

In a scientific paper bearing the admirably straightforward title "Use of Salt by Elk in Idaho," researchers Paul Dalke, Robert Beeman and others related the high points of the Nez Perce study results, in paraphrase to wit: Consumption of salt by elk was highest in spring (May and June), dropping off rapidly through the summer, becoming "nil" in late winter. Prior to mid-May, elk remained scattered, feeding on recent green-up vegetation, rather than congregating near salting stations. Primary forces working to hold naturally roaming elk in certain areas included lack of disturbance by people and cattle, choice vegetation and elevation— but not the presence or absence of salt. And finally, the Idaho elk preferred naturally occurring salt sources over artificial licks.

Although the researchers didn't say so, likely factors in the observed preference for natural salt sources include the presence of attractive trace minerals mixed with the naturally occurring salt, long-standing familiarity with natural salting sites and the greater seclusion, and thus security, of natural sites. Curiously, the majority of the preferred natural "licks" in the Idaho studies were in fact spring seeps; the elk weren't eating their salt so much as they were drinking it.

Additionally, the Idaho studies revealed—and no great surprise here—that where cattle, elk and deer come into competition for the same lick, might makes right, with cattle driving elk away and elk passing the buck along to deer. Similarly, within a given elk herd congregating around a lick, dominant bulls preferred the salt block itself to surrounding soil impregnated with salt dissolved from the block, prompting "much fighting" to establish salt-block dominance.

In sum, the authors concluded that "salt placed on summer range did not induce elk to remain longer or to leave winter range earlier."

Down here in southern Colorado, not so far from my own little shack and at the same elevation, a benign old gentleman named Lars long kept a small acreage, dragging a stumpy little travel trailer up every spring and parking it in the shimmering aspen shade and sitting there all day all summer every summer (for as long as he lasted) watching birds and other wild things come and go. It was in the mid-1970s, shortly before my advent here, that Lars started putting out salt to attract bigger beasties.

It took a while for night-roaming wapiti to locate the Lars lick (deer, being bolder users of "civilized" habitat, found it first) and to start visiting regularly, but gradually they did. By the time I came on the scene, both species of cervid had been hitting the lick long enough to have pawed and gnawed a soil crater four feet wide, eight feet long and two feet deep. Having no natural licks nearby, and with water all around, the animals obviously appreciated the fifty-pound trace-mineral salt blocks old Lars kept them supplied with.

For years I spied on Lars' lick more or less daily; even helped in his annual winter absences to keep it going. The results of this informal research were, to borrow an apt term from the Idaho re-searchers, "interesting." Confirming the Idaho findings, my local

Colorado elk, and mule deer as well, seemed to utilize the lick most intensely during late spring, only sporadically (and then mostly at night) during rut, while all but ignoring it in winter.

But then, given that Lars's place sits in a transitional zone between lower winter and higher summer elk ranges, we naturally *have* more elk here during late spring than at any other time of year. In winter, while visitation to the lick dropped off significantly, it nonetheless continued, with the few elk who hung high through the cold months occasionally pawing down through as much as two feet of snow to add a few grains of spice to their otherwise dreary winter diets.

Yet, the year-round availability of salt clearly did nothing whatsoever to *hold* elk up here at eight grand all wicked winter. Rather, it seemed that the hardy handful of wapiti wintering hereabouts merely visited the neighborhood lick in the course of their normal foraging rounds.

Alas, all of that is history now. Lars is gone and civilization has invaded. These days, the erstwhile lick is bracketed on the north by a two-story trophy home, on the east by a girl in a yurt with two big barky dogs. Caroline and I still occasionally walk that way, but we haven't seen an elk at the lick in several years now, and only rarely does a wandering muley leave its heart-shaped signature in the silted-in salt pit. Progress.

Whether in Colorado, Idaho or elsewhere, salt usage by elk seems to be an acquired taste—like Kona coffee, Irish whiskey and Cuban cigars among discerning humans—a luxury indulged in *when it's handy*, but lacking sufficient magnetism to alter natural elk distribution patterns—which, by and large, are dictated by the seasonal availability of the Big Four *necessities* of wapiti habitat: food, water, thermal and hiding cover and room to roam.

In his 1951 masterpiece, *Elk of North America*, Olaus J. Murie put forth (in a pleasantly roundabout fashion) an opinion similar to that formed independently by my former neighbor Lars, myself and the Idaho researchers—that while wild ungulates aren't *born* with an innate taste for salt, they can, given time and opportunity, come to value it. Murie postulates:

> It has been repeatedly noted that when salt has been made available to elk or moose, the animals have not been greatly attracted to it at first, although later they acquire a taste for it. An experiment conducted one winter on the National Elk Refuge in Jackson Hole, Wyoming, brought out this same reaction; and at the end of the winter it was found that the elk, several thousands of which were present, had consumed a relatively small amount of salt compared with what would have been taken by cattle.

Shifting to the question of whether or not putting out salt benefits wapiti health and happiness, Murie continues:

> It is true, of course, that wild animals that have become accustomed to eating salt continue to seek it eagerly and eat it with obvious relish. It may be well to tell here of a tame elk which had perfect freedom to range where it pleased, that was inordinately fond of tobacco and would eat cigarettes as long as they were given to him. Does it therefore follow that tobacco should have been provided for this animal as a necessary ration? So far, the evidence points to a sufficiency of mineral salts in [natural] elk forage. Well-meaning efforts to improve the condition of the elk by feeding salt may be simply introducing a new appetite that further study may show is useless, if not harmful, in the long run.

The Wildlife Management Institute's *Elk of North America: Ecology and Management* offers a more succinct, albeit less personable summary than Murie's:

> Salt use by elk, as with many other ungulate species, is primarily a habit-formed luxury. There is no doubt that Rocky Mountain

elk are attracted to salt; that they thrive without it seems equally certain. ... One comprehensive assessment [the Idaho studies] concluded that, as a means of altering the migratory habits of elk, the use of salt was ineffective. It was found, however, that as a means of inducing localized forage use, salt is perhaps one of few good attractants.

Sweeping all these scattered bits into a neat little pile, we can say with some confidence that while elk and other mammals, wild and domestic, need minimal amounts of salt to maintain life and health, they/we clearly do not need or instinctively crave supplemental quantities. In elk, the taste for salt is acquired, seasonal and incidental.

As one who automatically sprinkles salt on his food even before tasting it—an unabashed chloride junkie—I envy elk their superhuman self-restraint.

Along Wapiti Trails

CAN'T REALLY SAY WHAT sent me up that tree, but the way things turned out, I was happy as a lark to be there.

I was hiking a heavily forested, north-facing mountain slope a few miles from my shotgun shack, climbing toward an elk wallow in a secluded aspen bowl I'd stumbled into the year before. Camouflaged and moving as quietly as an impatient modern man can manage, I took my sweet old time closing the last stretch to the wallow, where I peeked over the final rise and saw ... nothing. The wallow was still there (no loggers or livestock or ATVs had come berserking through to destroy it), and active at that—the little pool of water in its center was clouded, and big cloven hoof prints pocked its muddy perimeter. But no visible life nowhere.

It was a pretty, peaceful place in which to invest a few hours of my life, and I was nosing around for a reasonably comfortable, well-hidden spot to sit and wait and watch when I happened to look up and see the tree stand—a small plywood platform chained fifteen feet up an old-growth fir. The long-ago hunter who'd hung that stand had picked the perfect tree, rooted as it was twenty yards from the wallow and directly over the primary game trail dropping into the marshy bowl from a sprawling aspen grove above.

The stand's splintered, weathered appearance testified to its long abandonment to the public domain, strengthening my hope that nobody but me knew about or visited this high hidden place. An urge for upward mobility struck, and skyward I went, climbing easily up a well-spaced ladder of rusted spike nails driven deep into the big tree.

After testing the strength of the platform—a bit wobbly but seemingly safe—I stepped gingerly aboard and, minding my balance, peeled off my pack. Before hanging the pack from a handy limb stump, I retrieved a length of nylon rope, wrapped it two turns around the tree and myself and secured the make-do safety harness with a Boy Scout bowline, in case I should fall asleep.

I had just taken a seat on the splintery platform, legs dangling, and was enjoying the view when my peripheral vision caught a flicker of fur slipping along the game trail above me. Whatever it was—big, but indecipherable behind the screen of trees— would round a bend and come eye-level with me at any moment. Hardly believing my luck, I imagined a beautiful big bull passing directly below me on his way to the wallow. Not many folks, aside from the relatively few elk hunters who use tree stands, have observed elk antlers from such an angelic angle.

But what it was, was two hundred pounds and more of bear, a young male judging by the big-headed, big-footed, lanky looks of him. The force of the adrenaline flood almost washed me out of the tree.

This bruin shuffling my way, I noted, like most "black" bears I've met across my years roaming these southern Rockies, had not a speck of black on him. His torso was sandy brown with darker legs and head and—unique in my experience—a wide blond stripe running the full length of his back, giving him the comical appearance of a behemoth skunk. With every padded step, the big bruin uttered a soft guttural grunt, as if it hurt to walk, or else felt really good; hard to say which.

Within spitting range up the hill from my tree, a big old spruce had fallen across the trail, its belly lodged about three feet above the ground. Coming to this minor obstacle, the bear paused to reconnoiter. Suddenly his head shot up and his ears went erect. I hadn't set foot anywhere near that log and there wasn't a breath of breeze, yet the bear had obviously caught a whiff of something he didn't much like. I couldn't help but to take it personal. After a full minute of alert indecision, the bear squeezed beneath the log and continued on down the trail. Then, directly at the base of my tree, he stopped again.

When sneaking around in the woods, as I do almost daily, looking to find and not be found, I wear scent-proof rubber-bottom boots spiced with diluted elk urine, full-body camouflage laundered in unscented soda ash and hung out nightly to air, and strive never to step on, sit on or touch anything unnecessarily. Even so, that two-hundred pound nose down there had caught my whiff and tracked my scent trail right up the tree until, inevitably, our eyes met—small, inscrutable eyes (his), lustrous amber ingots set in a head big enough to stuff a five-gallon bucket. His paws were wider than my boots, his claws overdue for a trim. As always at such intense, intimate times, I squinted to hide the bloody whites of my own eyes, even as I dared not blink, sneeze or fart and struggled to control, to conceal, the bellows-pumping of my lungs, the kettle-drum booming of my heart. Almost like being in love.

While I hunt every year for my little family's meat, I don't hunt bears. Though I rarely think in such dreamy terms, I suppose I could say that bears are my spiritual totems. At the least, they are my silent comrades in the living forest, loners and opportunists like me; threatened like me by the destruction of the wild, fearful (like me) of man yet potentially fierce and manlike in many ways, doglike in others. No matter how many I see, I never see bears enough, and to hunt them is simply unthinkable.

But what, I considered that day—being treed, as it were—what if the bear should decide to hunt *me*?

I've heard first-hand accounts—from a reformed bear guide and others—of the speed and ferocity with which an adult black bear can come up a tree after a man (or, should it be the case, a woman) when, as happens on rare occasion, one takes a notion to do so. And me sitting there literally tied in place, my "hunting" knife (never hunted nothing with it, in fact) somewhere in my pack, out of immediate reach and of little likely use in any event.

Strange, paranoid thoughts, I suppose, yet these were the thoughts I was thinking as I traded close stares with an unpredictable predatory carnivore who outweighed me by at least fifty pounds and carried far superior armament and likely superior intelligence.

By this time my heart had climbed into my throat and was trying, like some evil alien infant, to rip its way out. Chances are, I could simply have yelled and waved my arms and the bear would have acted from instinct and run. But this was no time for chance: What if his reaction was fight rather than flight? Nor, in any event, could I bring myself to smash the spell, to murder the moment.

So I did nothing.

The bear, still standing directly below me, now and then shifted its gaze down to the wallow with its muddy little pool of water. It was a warm September afternoon and the bruin clearly was thirsty; maybe even wanted a nice cool swim (I've seen it before, from close enough to be splashed; but that's another story). Yet, that infallible nose smelled trouble lurking, and had a good notion as to just where that trouble sat perched. Again he looked up and straight into my eyes. Again I sat still as stone and met his stare with a squint.

After some ten minutes of this—a very long time, it seemed at the time—the bear came of a sudden to a decision, shot me one last doleful, disdainful look, uttered a disgruntled *whoof*, spun around, squeezed back under the blowdown log and shambled away, following the same well-worn game trail that had brought him to me. This miles-long slope of mountains is sprinkled with springs, and he'd go find one less crowded.

As is always the way at the conclusion of such close, potentially dangerous ursine encounters, it was with a tumultuous tangle of grief and relief that I watched him go—a wise, cautious fellow, a "good bear" as it turned out. As most by nature are. I waited and watched for several minutes more before climbing down from my tree and scurrying like a chipmunk out of there.

As I loped down the mountain in failing light—moving quickly but quietly, peering around intently, happily hyper-alert because my route, of necessity, loosely paralleled the departing bear's—I felt I knew what life is all about. Once again, my mostly mundane existence had been visited by an ancient ineffable magic. For an unforgettable little while, on a perfect September evening, my "inner predator" had become potential prey.

Such gifts of nature have come my way many's the time before, and more are out there waiting; you only have to meet them halfway. The perfectly precise, utterly equitable, happily humbling, role-reversing irony of such natural juxtapositions as meeting a bear in the woods, one on one, go a far piece (if you think about it hard enough, long enough) toward helping us to answer (each for his or her ownself, as ultimately it must be) the Big Questions—to grasp the meanings of life and death and conquer our fears of both.

The answers are out there—sweet as the song of a canyon wren, clear as mountain water, obvious as the antlers on a bull elk's head—it's just that for the past few thousand years or so, we've been aiming too high, looking in all the wrong places.

Halfway down the mountain, my searching eyes stuck fast to an artful arrangement of white, glowing eerily in the soft golden tint of twilight. At first, incongruous as it seemed, I took it for a pile of broken china. Of course I dodged over to check it out, and found no cast-off litter of china, but the fully articulated, cleanly bleached skeleton of an adult coyote. The bones remained in a lifelike configuration, still loosely connected with shreds of pink cartilage, rather than having been scattered by scavengers, including of course other coyotes, as per the norm. Certainly, the flesh had been consumed by *something*—birds, perhaps, bugs and bacteria for sure—but nothing big and powerful enough to rip limb from torso and scatter the leftovers about. I stooped and stared and studied, at first without touching, thinking to leave the skeletal sculpture be. And then I noticed the skull.

Just above and behind the yawning left eye socket were two small round holes. When I picked up the skull, the lower jaw detached and lay like a toothy wishbone in my hand. The teeth, I noted, all were clean and sharp and strong, implying a youthful adult. This animal, in all likelihood, had not perished of old age (in the wild, few do). Placing the jaw above the skull, I noted that the pair of holes in the skull matched perfectly, in both spacing and diameter, with the erstwhile coyote's lower canines. Clearly, another coyote had bitten clean through this unfortunate creature's skull and into its brain case. The question, the curiosity, thus became and remains: Did this violent intrusion happen before, thus causing, this fellow's death ... or after? And in either event, *why?*

How deadly dull our lives would be, devoid of natural mystery!

Across those wonderful weeks of prowling the mountain forests that autumn (not so long ago, and like so many others), I enjoyed additional adventures ... including a couple more close-ups with bears ... an impromptu encounter with a pine marten—a big, beautiful, catlike weasel with a gorgeous burnt-auburn coat— who allowed me to stand for minutes, just a few yards away, as it nosed back and forth along a deadfallen aspen, searching excitedly for a chink in the aspen's armor, an opening large enough to allow it to squeeze inside the hollow heart and munch the terrified rodent quivering therein ... the abrupt and definitive death squeaks of white-footed mice, seven in all and all within an hour one cold early morning, as a female long-tailed weasel slew the rodents serially, following the briefest of back-to-back hunts, packing the wee warm corpses, one at a time, right past my boots on the way back to feed her ravenous den ... big, bold ravens—different birds on different days in separate places—who tipped me to approaching elk ... and more.

And through it all, in memory as in fact, meander wapiti trails.

A Tribute

AS YOU MIGHT EXPECT of a girl who was raised from age nine in the rowdy far-north outpost of Fairbanks, Alaska, in the opening decades of the century, and who went on to become the first female graduate of the University of Alaska—as you might expect, Margaret Elizabeth Thomas was quite the spirited young lady.

Appropriately, "Mardy" Thomas would meet and marry quite the spirited young man—Olaus J. Murie, an adventurous field biologist destined to become, among many another accomplishment, the "father of modern elk management."

In her lively and nostalgic first book, a memoir titled *Two in the Far North* (1962), Mardy recalls her premiere meeting with Olaus, in 1921. He was, she wrote, "a slim blond young man, not handsome in my schoolgirl eyes, but with the freshest complexion and the bluest eyes." After she'd come to know him better, Mardy's admiration of Olaus went more than skin deep: "Here," she observed, "was a man, gentle but with steel in him."

Olaus Johan Murie, of hardy Norwegian stock, was born in Minnesota in 1889, earned bachelor's and master's degrees in biology, conducted graduate field research in Hudson Bay, Canada, and served in the Army Air Corps during World War I. In 1920, Murie joined the U.S. Biological Survey (now the U.S. Fish and Wildlife Service) and was promptly dispatched to Alaska. By the time he met Mardy, Olaus had already been "in country" long enough to become widely respected as a field biologist, federal game warden and master woodsman.

Following a courtship complicated by long separations—he in the bush, she away at school—Olaus and Mardy were married in November, 1924. By way of a honeymoon, the Muries embarked on a physically brutal scientific expedition, traveling at first by riverboat, then, with the onset of the subarctic winter, 550 miles by dog sled into the Brooks Range, there to study caribou and acquire (that is, shoot) museum specimens. Along the way, the newlyweds regularly bivouacked trail-side in apparent comfort and with great good cheer—in temperatures as lung-sucking cold as thirty below nothing.

"What more could a young bride ask?" is how Mardy, apropos, recalls that wild and woolly honeymoon.

In 1927, after six years of field work in Alaska and the Yukon, documenting the lives of creatures as mighty as the brown bear (grizzly), as diminutive as mice (an important food for wolves, among others), Olaus was transferred to western Wyoming, on the eastern flank of the majestic Teton Range of the Rocky Mountains, there to study the elk of Jackson Hole. In *Wapiti Wilderness* (1966), co-authored by the Muries, Olaus summarized the problems that brought them there:

> The elk herd, estimated at about 20,000 animals, the largest herd in the world, seemed to have fallen on evil times. ... There had been a great deal of newspaper and magazine publicity about "the starving elk of Jackson Hole." The Izaak Walton League of America [and other conservation groups] were all raising money with which to purchase private lands to be added to the already established National Elk Refuge adjoining the town of Jackson ... so that there would be more forage for the elk when they came down from the hills in winter. Finally the President had appointed a national "Elk Commission" to correlate the existing information and to make recommendations. One of the recommendations was that the Bureau of Biological Survey assign a research biologist to do a thorough study of the life history of the elk and every factor affecting their welfare, this study to take whatever length

of time was needed to make it complete. This was just the kind of free yet demanding assignment I loved.

It didn't take long to literally step into the problem, with Olaus complaining to Margaret on their first field trip that the country was so "tracked up" with cattle that the mess they left behind seriously hindered his ability to conduct elk research.

Across the next several years, Murie's exhaustive studies of the Jackson elk herd earned him international recognition, as he methodically, and courageously, went about documenting and exposing the culprits, including the fragmenting of critical wildlife range into fenced pastures, the grazing-off of prime elk forage, the extermination of wolves and grizzlies—the natural predators which for millennia had culled elk herds of their marginalia and, thus, helped to shape the grand cervid species we know today—and various diseases attributable to a cow-burnt habitat.

For a telling instance: The most troublesome of the several diseases infecting Jackson Hole wapiti was "sore mouth," which erupts when elk are forced to subsist on coarse and unsuitable forage—most often, noxious non-native weeds introduced by livestock—the leftovers after cattle or sheep have gleaned the cream. Writing again in *Wapiti Wilderness*, Olaus summarized the "elk problem":

> In those days there was bounteous summer range for elk and cattle. It was after the hunting season, after the bulk of the herd had drifted down out of the deep snow country to the valley floor, that the elk fell on evil times. And my days became busier, more strenuous.
>
> If the winter was a hard one and the elk were more concentrated on the fields of the Refuge, then we would begin to find elk lying dead or dying. I watched them as they lay. I watched them as they died. I did a post-mortem examination of each one if I could. One dreadful winter, 1,175 died on the fields of the Refuge. ...

I had found that the elk who died—the great proportion of them, at any rate—were dying [of the disease] *necrotic stomatitis.* ... The bacillus that causes this infection is present everywhere, especially on the winter feed grounds of the Refuge, where the elk become concentrated. It needs only a lesion in the membranes of the mouth, throat, tongue, or gums to become lodged and set up its infection, and the lesions are caused by any unusually sharp awn in hay or grass, such as foxtail grass, or by sharp coarse fibers of willow or other browse too coarse to be easily chewed.

The course of the disease is similar to pneumonia. After the elk get too weak to stand or eat, they are doomed to die in about twenty-four hours.

There were other facets to this disease, of course, and other diseases and other factors, but this was the main cause of the elk problem.

Outlining his solutions to the Jackson area's wapiti woes, Murie continued:

Almer [Nelson, the Refuge manager] and I figured out a safe carrying capacity for the winter range; a program of eradication of foxtail hay on Refuge lands was begun. ... Most important, the State of Wyoming and the federal government were able to acquire more lands to be added to the Refuge so that there is more room for the elk to spread out and to seek their own natural forage. Besides all this, Almer started a program of leaving some of the cultivated hayfields uncut. The animals could then spread out and seek their own food further into the winter months.

The robust health of the Jackson herd today, and of the Refuge, which, as the millennium approaches, sustains ten to twelve thousand elk through each brutal northern winter, speaks of Murie's wisdom and courageous leadership at a critical juncture.

In 1937, the Muries joined the Wilderness Society, a leading conservation organization then as now. In 1946 (the year I came screaming and kicking into this bloody lovely world), Olaus was invited to become the Society's director. With Mardy's encouragement, he agreed—but only on condition that he could remain in Jackson Hole rather than relocate to the Society's Washington, D.C., headquarters. A compromise was reached wherein the Society settled for a half-time director, Olaus for half pay, allowing the Muries to continue their active outdoor lives in their beloved wapiti wilderness.

At this happy juncture, finding himself no longer in censorious government service and with more time to himself, Olaus took up serious writing. In 1951, the Wildlife Management Institute published Murie's wapiti magnum opus, *Elk of North America*, in whose 376 pages the author shares his unparalleled knowledge and, even more important, understanding of and empathy for elk.

In a foreword to that work, then-WMI President Ira M. Gabrielson hailed *Elk of North America* as "the first comprehensive treatise on this noble American animal based on adequate field study ... the result of years of tireless field work by Olaus J. Murie, one of the world's top field naturalists. ... This volume is, and will be for a long time, the last word on the behavior and characteristics of the elk."

And "for a long time" indeed it was, reigning as the elkheart's bible for thirty-one years, until 1982, when it was superseded by an exhaustive scientific anthology of the same name, edited by Jack Ward Thomas, the future (then) and former (now) chief of the U.S. Forest Service, and Dale E. Toweill.

As if adventurer, biologist, wildlife management reformer and writer weren't enough, Murie was also a singularly talented wildlife artist. As the illustrious Roger Tory Peterson points out in his editor's introduction to the second edition of Murie's *A Field Guide to Animal Tracks* (1954): "Olaus Murie reminds us very much of an earlier master, Ernest Thompson Seton. Like Seton, he was not only an eminent naturalist and an accomplished woodsman, but also a fine artist, able to interpret in pen and ink the things he had witnessed."

Finally and most fundamentally, Olaus Murie was a dedicated conservationist. Consequently, in his new position of influence as director of the Wilderness Society, one of Murie's first campaigns was against the government-sponsored war on predators— among the earliest and still today the most insidious of the endless tax-funded subsidies to the western public-lands welfare ranching scam. This, however, was not a battle even Murie, or for that matter and to date, anyone, could win. Under the U.S. Department of Agriculture's Animal Services branch (formerly Animal Damage Control, and before that Predator and Rodent Control), the publicly subsidized killing of "animals injurious to agriculture" continues to this day, though often clearly detrimental to elk and other vegetarian wildlife.

The Muries did, however, prevail on other important fronts, such as halting yet another damning [*sic*] of the Colorado River, which would have flooded much of priceless Dinosaur National Monument in Colorado and Utah for (again!) private agricultural profit.

But the Muries' most difficult and rewarding environmental battle was their long- and hard-fought effort to establish a huge and ecologically imperative wildlife refuge in their beloved Alaska, culminating in a 1960 victory. In 1959, you'll recall, Alaska became America's forty-ninth state; the following year, the nine-million-acre Arctic National Wildlife Refuge was set aside.

In poignant retrospect, Mardy recalls the moment she and Olaus first learned of this triumph, climaxing years of strenuous lobbying: "Olaus was at his table at the back of the room, writing. I held out the telegram to him; he read it and stood and took me in his arms and we both wept."

Olaus Murie continued to *live* until he died—of cancer, in 1963, at the age of seventy-four. To posterity he left a tremendously expanded knowledge of elk and elk management, a larger and healthier National Elk Refuge in Wyoming, an intact Dinosaur National Monument in Colorado and Utah, a national treasure in the form of the Arctic National Wildlife Refuge in Alaska and, with plenty of help from Mardy, three fine children and four timeless volumes of autobiographical natural history (the best kind).

Today, well into her nineties, Margaret Murie remains quite the spirited young lady—still energetic and active, still ensconced in the comfortable log cabin at Moose, Wyoming, which she and Olaus first occupied back in 1945. Of her late husband she has written:

> He had a very dedicated and keen curiosity about everything that ever walked or crawled or lived. That was his motivating force— to find out more. He used to say that there is no limit to man's capacity to learn things, if man didn't destroy himself first by destroying his earth.

That race—which Albert Einstein described as a contest between knowledge and disaster—may be in the final lap even now, with disaster in the lead. Yet there is hope: In 1998, in recognition of her decades of heartfelt effort on behalf of America's public lands, Margaret Murie was awarded the Presidential Medal of Freedom.

It seems appropriate to end this inadequate tribute with words from "the father of modern elk management" himself, lifted from the closing paragraphs of his *Elk of North America*:

To a large class of individuals, part of the value of the elk is its ecological significance, although they may not express it in those words. Elk trails leading to natural licks have more significance and much more interest than a group of elk at a block of salt put out in a meadow. ... [This and more is all] part of a complex story in natural history that has great educational value and interest. ...

Fortunately, many elk ranges are still in fairly primitive state and the values indicated above have not been destroyed. Looking to the future, in view of the needs of elk and the exacting requirements of recreation based on multiple use, the safest course is to model elk management along natural lines, not only to preserve the elk as a living animal, but also, so far as is reasonably possible, to preserve its distinctive habits as well as its habitat.

Indeed, we can hardly have one without the other.

Bugged

TYPICALLY FOR LATE August hereabouts, the wapiti and I are slouching through a hot, dry, somnolent afternoon. Swarms of big, blue-green iridescent flies have just driven me out of a damp, shady hollow where I'd planned to spend the siesta hours spying on a stinky-fresh wallow. I stood it as long as I could, but the flies finally won, swarming me like something fresh out of the smarter end of a sheep. For their part, the elk are bedded I know not where, and likely no less bugged.

Since I've hiked all the long way here—high in a local but heretofore unexplored (by me) mountain range—in hopes of seeing, or at least hearing elk, and (as usual) lacking any brighter idea, I decide to invest what's left of the afternoon insinuating myself into the neighborhood of a husky-sounding bull who bugled a couple of times at sunrise this morning. Catch is, those bugles bellowed up from somewhere down near the bottom of this mountain I'm now standing atop. My task, then, is to guesstimate the bull's approximate location and navigate myself to directly (more or less) above him with the help of midday upslope thermals, and do so without being so noisy or clumsy as to jump him out of his day bed. That done, I'll be in position to sneak in close enough for a good long look-and-listen should he start mouthing-off again this evening.

Complicating this caper is that this is *terra incognita* to me. I hitched a twelve-mile horsey ride to camp yesterday with a couple of biologist friends come to electrocute native cutthroat trout in a remote creek and count their little carcasses, most of which in fact will revive and survive. Had a bit too much to drink last night, one too many cigars (the norm when camping with cowboys), but dutifully arose and hauled my hangover up here in the wee hours of the morning. My companions, meanwhile, went tracking after the half-dozen equine imbeciles who wandered— rather, hop-scotched—off sometime during the night, *way* off, it seems, blithely ignoring their hobbled front hooves.

Consequently, I barely know where the hell I am. And consequent to consequence, getting myself to where I think I want to be—where I think the bull may be—then getting back to camp from there, in the dark, is going to require a sweet little piece of map-and-compass work. But hey, I'm a Marine; I'll either do it or croak trying. The flies, in fact, seem to think I'm already carrion. Dead meat walking.

Slouching along far less cautiously than one who wishes to put the sneak on wary wildlife should—it's just too damn hot to get into much of a weaseling mood, exacerbated by the flipping flies, who keep my hands windmilling—I slop over the lip of the mountain's evergreen-bearded north face and crunch a couple hundred yards down into the dense, dark conifer forest. Spying a comfortable-looking patch of spruce needles in a tiny clearing in the shade, I peel off my sweat-soaked pack and plop down for a snack and a spell of reconnoitering; wouldn't really care to get seriously lost up here in this maze of mountains, so many steep miles from the nearest road or trail.

The crisp new USGS map sheet unfolds with a rattle, warning all creatures great and small of my rude intrusion. Whether or not the map will get me where I want to go, then back to camp, I can't yet say—there are few laudable landmarks in this heavily wooded, steeply corrugated terrain—but the map serves well enough to fan the flies off my sandwich. After crudely determining my position, the morning bugler's likely location and an appropriate compass course, I refold the map, *crinkle-crinkle*, and slip it back into my pack.

Feeling an urgent pressure in my bladder and not wishing to attract even more flies to my shady rest, I stand, stretch and stroll off a ways. As I gaze blankly about, just hanging out, my attention is caught by a flicker of movement a little down the slope. Staring, I gradually discern what appears, like an animate Rorschach test, to be the head and neck of a cow elk bedded in the shade of a fir. Maybe forty yards.

My business finished, I slink back a couple of paces and sink to my knees ... bring up the binoculars that dangle always from my red (sunburnt) neck and confirm what my disbelieving eyes are reporting. Sure enough, there lies a cow elk, grandly grinding cud, paying my rude intrusion not a cent of attention.

Most curious: How could a sharp-sensed wapiti not have seen, heard or smelt my careless approach? How could I have sat for so long in plain sight—eating lunch, drinking from a big white-plastic water bottle, rattling and waving around a noisy, white-backed map sheet, swatting flies, rising and walking and standing and pissing—making all that commotion without her ever noticing me?

I am at first dumbfounded, but a few minutes of glassing exposes the answer: flies. The bedded cow continually and frantically twitches her ears, shakes her head, jerks and twists convulsively to bite at her hindquarters in a fruitless attempt to shoo the pesky little turd-eaters away. But all for naught. No sooner does her head go down to attempt a nap, then it snaps back up, ears all a'twitch.

Now the cow stands and shakes like a wet dog. Walks around a little. Beds again. Is swarmed anew by the buzzing bastards. My heart goes out (as per the gruesome cliché) to the poor, handless, tail-less beast (a few inches of stub there, but worthless as a swatter).

I knee-crawl back to my pack, shift around until I find a good spying spot and settle in for a spell of eyeballing the dense woods around and downslope from the cow; where one elk is bedded, especially this time of year, more are almost certain to be nearby.

Alas, after a good long look—having spied no more wapiti and with the flies distracting me almost as much as they are that woebegone cow down there—I determine that I have nothing to lose by pushing my luck a little, see how close I can get. So I rise to my knees, pull on my pack, stand and start down the slope, hoping to circumnavigate the cow undetected and find a more advantageous vantage from which to glass a fresh chunk of scenery; see what turns up.

What turns up, before I've taken even a dozen steps, is the big beige rump of a second bedded beast. I sneak that way.

It's another cow ... and just beyond, a big calf. More cows. Now a spike bull jumps up from an unseen bed—not because I've spooked him; like the rest of the universe, he has no idea I exist—shakes violently, sprints into a leafy patch of oak brush, flails around a bit with adolescent antlers then bolts off again, this time plum out of sight; a one-animal stampede. Like a wake behind a boat, his trail is marked in the air by a line of jilted flies in hot pursuit.

And so it goes for the better part of three of the most amazing hours I've ever spent out amongst the elk. And I do mean amongst. Thanks more to the flippin' flies than to any skills I may possess as a stalker, I'm able to spend the whole afternoon floating like a bearded ghost through a scattered and terminally distracted herd of a dozen or so cows, calves and (briefly) that gone-postal spike bull.

At one point I find myself trading stares with a yearling cow from an incredible five yards—standing behind a screen of brush, she's caught me red-faced tiptoeing along atop a fallen log (quieter than walking on the crunchy forest duff). But I hold her interest only momentarily, then the sorrowful soul is buzz-bombed anew by flies and returns to jerking, twitching and pacing about. As with all her mates, the little cow's normally foolproof cervid senses seem to have been short-circuited by this nonpareil blight of bugs. And though they evidence a slight preference for elk flesh over human, we suffer together, the wapiti and me. Fair enough.

During a short spell of sitting and watching, the notion enters what's left of my mind that if a clumsy human predator can move with virtual impunity among a herd of elk thanks to the acute distraction of swarming flies, likewise could a cougar, a bear, a wolf. In fact, across the ages, I'd bet Caroline's best china that many an elk has died just that way. This way. Clearly, swarming biting buzzing bugs create not just a bothersome nuisance to elk, but a real and present danger, providing as they do a maddening distraction that makes the work of predators infinitely easier.

And sometimes, the bugs themselves are the predators, the killers and consumers of elk.

I think of the green-headed horsefly and its bloody conspirator, the sorehead roundworm—*Elaeophora schneideri*. Fortunately for elk, the range of the latter is limited pretty much to the extreme southern Rockies. The worst problems have occurred in the Gila Wilderness and Gila National Forest in southwestern New Mexico, and the Apache-Sitgreaves National Forest in southeastern Arizona. In these places, elaeophorosis—known as "sorehead" to sheepmen (takes one to know one)—occasionally wreaks havoc among elk and the privately owned domestic sheep that infest public-lands elk habitat. To a lesser degree, elaeophorosis has also been known to attack elk at Ted Turner's Vermejo Park Ranch in northern New Mexico, where the disease was studied by elk biologist (and, as of 1998, Rocky Mountain Elk Foundation president) Dr. Gary Wolfe.

In addition to severe external infections of the faces and foreheads of its victims, elaeophorosis produces symptoms similar to those of locoweed poisoning—lethargy, weight loss, lack of co-ordination, deformed antlers and clear-eyed blindness.

The primary host of *E. schneideri* is the mule deer, and the transmitter of the deadly parasite is the green-headed horsefly (*Hybomitra sonomensis*). Thus, elaeophorosis can become a significant threat only when elk, mule deer and *H. sonomensis* are concentrated together during the spring horsefly season.

In a normal scenario, the green-headed horsefly ingests the larvae of the sorehead roundworm while feeding on the blood of an infected mule deer. Following the two weeks it takes the larvae to develop into subadult *E. schneideri* inside the fly, the tiny predators are transmitted to wapiti via a bite. The favored victims of elaeophorosis—as with most predators of elk and as natural selection deems appropriate—are newborn calves.

Once *E. schneideri* invades a mammal's bloodstream, it "swims" to a carotid (neck) or cerebral (head) artery, where it sets anchor for the duration. The growing *E. schneideri*—and following its death, the calcified corpse—does its damage by gradually and increasingly obstructing blood flow to the victim's brain. Thus, an infected animal will die either by stroke or, after being blinded by the disease, become easy prey to predators, starvation or accident.

Of course and thankfully, these elk I'm spying on now show no sign of disease—these aren't horseflies pestering us, but common cow-pie connoisseurs. I swat at one, just miss, and wonder: Has it been like this for these elk—the flies, and the misery, distraction and danger they bring—every hot, humid afternoon this entire rainy summer long? And other summers stretching back into antiquity? If so, and it probably is so, the beleaguered elk have my empathy. I plop down on a rock and fall to musing.

Specifically: The wapiti "literature" contains less than a wealth of insight into the testy relationship between elk and flies. Still,

some interesting observations have been recorded. In the original
Elk of North America, Olaus J. Murie's comments on flies and
elk conveniently corroborate my own observations, and possibly
yours:

> During summer, notably in July and part of August, the actions
> of a band of elk resting in a meadow plainly indicate that the an-
> imals are considerably annoyed by flies—horseflies, deer flies and
> others. The elk shake their heads, flap their ears and otherwise
> try to get rid of their tormentors. Frequently an elk gets up,
> walks about and then lies down again, unable to keep still in the
> presence of these biting pests. Under similar conditions horses
> find some relief by going into shade, and to some extent the elk
> appear to follow that practice. ... There, in the shady interior of
> thickets that the flies appear to shun to some extent, the elk ob-
> tain a degree of freedom from the flies.

Earlier in the century, in his four-volume classic, *Lives of Game
Animals*, artist-naturalist-hunter Ernest Thompson Seton related
anecdotal evidence of wapiti fly-avoidance techniques far more
imaginative than merely shading-up. Under the heading "Insect
Terrors," Seton wrote ...

> The creatures that [the elk] really dreads are the living things with
> wings and stings, that assail him in baffling, irresistible millions
> and drive him to the refuge of high hills, deep water or armour
> made of mud. J. K. Lord, writing of the wild life in the West
> (1866), says: "Travelling in Oregon, one constantly finds oneself
> on the banks of a wide glassy lake; gazing over its unrippled sur-
> face, the eye suddenly rests on what to the inexperienced in
> hunter's craft, appears to be small clumps of twisted branches, or
> dead and leafless tree-tops, the trunks of which are hidden in the
> water; but the Indian and trapper discerns in a second that the
> apparent branches are the antlers of a herd of Wapiti that has
> been driven into the water by flies."

Yet, among all documented techniques employed by elk to avoid flies and other flying, biting bugs, the most common and effective is not aping hippos, but retreating to the cool relief of high, chill, windswept timberline meadows. Of course, what share of the drive among elk for summertime upward mobility is fueled by insects, and what owes to their appetite for the nutritious, late-greening alpine forage available there—not to mention the blessed quiet and privacy, miles from roads and human ruckus—is open to investigation.

Seton's suggestion that elk sometimes coat themselves with an "armour made of mud" against biting flies is, in my experience, questionable. The "evidence" for anti-bug mud-bathing appears to be wholly anecdotal. In any event, should such behavior in fact exist, "mudding" cannot be equated with the wallowing of rutting bulls. The latter is complex and far from totally understood, yet it's doubtful that wallowing has much if anything to do with insect avoidance—especially given that the bull urinates in the mud before he rolls in it, which bestial behavior would run counter to fly avoidance. Even so, the dark, mud-caked hides of wallowing bull elk likely account for the anecdotal, antiquated "bug-armour made of mud" myth.

Another variety of insect-avoidance behavior among elk is reported in the current incarnation of *Elk of North America*. Therein, a contributing biologist reports from the Yellowstone area that, "Some elk at lower elevations apparently attempted to avoid insect attacks by bedding down in tall sedge meadows." This tidbit leaves me curious and wishing the writer had gone on to offer an explanation, or at least a hypothesis, for how sedge meadows may offer relief from insects. Mosquitoes, at least, love such swampy places.

But no matter, I guess, since there are no sedge meadows anywhere near this high dry Colorado mountain slope I'm presently haunting. And these elk I'm shadowing are a thousand feet below and miles away from the nearest windswept timberline promontory. Moreover, the largest body of water hereabouts is the ankle-deep trout brook down in the valley, presently being electrified by my camp comrades (assuming they found our missing mounts). Thus, "my" wapiti are left to twitch ears and shake hides, bite frantically at the jet-fast flies and piston up and down from their nests in tortured frustration—while a potentially deadly predator lurks oh so near, looking on.

Still, for all their bugged misery, these elk appear sleek, healthy, roundly rotund. Again, Murie's observations preconfirm my own. "The elk," wrote Olaus half a century ago, "seem resigned to the flies and take them as a matter of course. In fact, the animals do well and become fat during the fly season, a period of abundant and nourishing food."

🍂

The remainder of the day flies by, time confused and compressed by a prolonged adrenaline rush, and I never do make it down the mountain after that daybreak bull. I'm having too much fun, learning too much, thinking too much (as usual, quantity over quality) to abandon this fly-bit cervid circus.

But this too does finally pass, and after a pleasant but uneventful downhill twilight trip of a few fast miles, I reach camp just after dark. Here, with dinner sizzling over glowing campfire coals and the flies gone to ground (or wherever it is they go at night), a couple of cups of George Dickel and branch-water down the hatch, a good cheap Rum Crook clamped in my teeth, I descend once again into the murky depths of reflection, this time mentally muddling the role insect pests have played—and continue to play—in the ongoing drama of evolution. In due time, this looping line of thought leads me (once again) back to a telling scene from my late Montana friend A. B. Guthrie, Jr.'s masterful novel of the fur-trade era, *The Big Sky*. Along the banks of the mighty Missouri, Guthrie's 1830s mountain men curse their buggy fate:

> "Worse'n chiggers," Jim said, "these damn gnats. They don't serve no purpose, unless to remind a man he ain't such a somebody. I bet they figure we're made special for them. I bet they're sayin' thank you, God, for everything, only why did You have to put hands on a man, or a tail on a cow?

Or flapping ears and long dense hair and a tough thick hide on a wapiti. In the big picture, who's bugging whom, I reckon, is a matter of perspective.

The Bear Who Came to Dinner

WALKING ALONE IN the June woods, just nosing along, I round a bend in the game trail I'm following and almost step into a fresh, green-black bear flop, big and shiny as life itself. Black bear, obviously, given that grizzlies have been conspicuously absent in the immediate hereabouts for some time now. Not, I don't believe, utterly extinct, but plenty scarce after a century and a half of bloody persecution by ranchers and their Animal Damage Control quislings at the Department of Agriculture.

Ursus americanus—literally, "American bear," known popularly and confusingly as the "black" bear ... my old good friend, we meet again. Almost.

"Black" bear is an unfortunate choice of names for *U. americanus*, bestowed long ago by some provincial easterner, where most black bears in fact are black. But across its expansive North American range, the species comprises almost infinite color possibilities, especially in the West. Here in the bear-spangled mountains of southern Colorado, shades of brown are dominant— brown-brown and black-brown and tan-brown—plus cinnamon, yellow, white and often a multicolor patchwork. Across the years here, I've seen many non-black "black" bears for every true

113

blackie. Even in the eastern hardwood forests, many if not most black bears wear a blaze of white on chest or throat.

Another regional variant is size. Eastern bears run larger than their western counterparts. While Rocky Mountain males rarely exceed four-hundred pounds, six-hundred pound boars occasionally turn up in the Northeast. The largest black bear ever—killed in Wisconsin in 1885—flattened the scales at $802^{1/2}$ pounds—a rare huge monster even by grizzly standards. Female blackies average only 150 to 230 pounds here in the Rockies, up to around 350 in prime eastern habitat.

In addition to springtime elk calves and deer fawns, black bears prey opportunistically on rodents large and small, and occasionally snatch mid-sized livestock such as goats, sheep, beef calves and—that all-American breakfast—pork. And too, anything dead, the deader the better, is fair fare for a bear, especially during early spring when the bruins are just emerging, literally starved, from their winter dens and green-up is weeks yet away.

When shopping on the vegetable aisle, black bears are equally equitable, consuming forbs, berries, grasses, mast, sedges, herbaceous plants and the cambium of aspen and other soft-barked trees. For dessert there are insects (grasshoppers, I have it on good authority, taste "nutty"), honey and human garbage, including bear baits where such cowardly "sport" remains legal.

Black bears rarely pose a threat to humans—so long as they're treated with the respect due unto large, fast, well-armed, powerfully muscled, unpredictable meat-eating beasts. In fact, *wild* black bears—as opposed to brazen park beggars—are among the most reclusive of North American mammals and almost always will hightail it out of the neighborhood at the first whiff of human intrusion. *Almost* always.

Which is to say, there have been scores of people mauled by black bears in recent decades. And, as documented in Stephen

Herrero's eye-opening, heart-pounding *Bear Attacks*, some two dozen deaths. Most maulings occur when people attempt to pet, feed or harass habituated bears, though a few unfortunates, mostly children, have fallen victim to premeditated predation.

The best nonlethal defense against the rare bold bear (or cougar, or two-legged psycho) is hot-pepper spray. Lacking that, noisy aggression often works—yell, wave your arms, jump up and down, bang pots and pans, throw rocks or sticks, fire off a gun, etc. Unlike grizzlies, which evolved in open, treeless country with nowhere to run to, nowhere to hide, nothing to climb, and therefore were naturally selected in favor of an aggressive defense, black bears evolved in forests with abundant hiding cover, plenty trees to shinny up and, consequently, have adapted to flight over fight. Usually.

Most bears breed in June and July, with impregnated females enjoying delayed implantation until fall, at which time the fertilized egg attaches itself to the uterine wall and begins to grow. It's owing to this adaptive device, rather than happenstance, that cubs are conveniently born in den, usually during January or February.

In a marvelously adaptive species-survival caper, delayed implantation takes place only if the mother enjoyed a bountiful summer, packing on fat enough to assure the production of milk sufficient for the litter's survival without starving her to death. Otherwise, lacking that critical caloric "surplus," the pending pregnancy will self-destruct.

Once successfully hatched, baby blacks begin their careers as blind, fuzzy, utterly helpless half-pound ratballs. After nursing in den for a couple of months and achieving the great good weight of maybe five pounds, they follow their mother from the earthen winter womb out into a big bright world of adventure and risk.

Ironically, for most of their first summer, black bear cubs—like the elk calves and deer fawns they'll later transmogrify into bear

poop if given a chance—are themselves at significant risk of predation ... by males of their own species, by grizzlies, wolves,
wolverines, coyotes, cougars and many another hungry mouth.
But unlike elk calves, bear cubs readily climb trees and have
fiercely protective mothers armed with big sharp teeth and claws.

Bears: no forest without them holds much interest for me.

Naturally curious, I find a sturdy stick, kneel and commence
poking the poo—looking to see what this June bruin most recently enjoyed for dinner.

Inventory: The predictable stringers of half-digested grass and
other greens, a wad of crushed beetle carapace and a few unknown bone fragments. But wait: Down deep in the heart of the
heap, like some stinky Twinkie, hides a surprise. Two by two, I
pick out six small ebony jewels that, cleaned off a bit, become
three tiny deer hooves. The bear's enthusiastic digestive juices
have dissolved out the soft matrices, leaving only hard outer
shells of polished black keratin.

Obviously, the bear that passed these hooves while passing this
way either found and scavenged a dead fawn—or killed it himself. Or herself. No surprise in either event, since black bears,
like humans, are ravenously omnivorous and cleverly opportunistic; as Ernie Seton once stated the case, "a list of the Bear's
staples is not a list of what it likes, but of what it can get." In this
instance, it appears the bear liked what it got just fine, else he/she
wouldn't have gobbled it hooves and all.

Alas, I'll never know whether the bear killed or scavenged the
fawn; no amount of poking, snooping and sniffing could ever reveal that little secret of nature—but odds are soundly in favor of
predation since not all that many fawns are stillborn or die on

their own in fair weather, which we've recently had, and blackies are dedicated predators on the newborns of not only deer, but elk, moose, caribou and pronghorn.

And why not? Bears have been hunting elk far longer than you or I or even our most distant protohuman forebears; they've got first dibs. Besides, their annual productive elk-hunting season is little more than a month.

It's hard for most of us to admire, much less to excuse, a baby killer, and the overwhelming majority of elk killed by bears are calves just hours or days or, at most, a few weeks old. After that, healthy calves can run and dodge and leap like—well, like the deer they are—spending their days and nights surrounded by an attentive, protective nursery herd comprising a dozen or more, sometimes many more, cows and calves.

But for its first month or so, a wapiti calf's only defense against predation—by blackie, grizzly (where relict populations survive), wolf (ditto), coyote, cougar, bobcat, lynx, golden eagle, free-roaming (not necessarily feral) dogs et al.—the little critter's only defense against a world of hungry jaws is what biologists call the "hider strategy."

When her time draws near, a pregnant cow will wander away from the herd to a secluded nursery hide-out, usually in thick cover near abundant forage and water; aspen groves, where available, are greatly favored. There she'll give birth to her calf (only rarely calves), instinctively gobble up the mess and odor of afterbirth—then stroll off to graze, returning periodically to nurse and maybe move the wobbly babe to a fresh (odor free) spot.

During these long and frequent separations from its mother, a newborn calf instinctively lies still as a stone and flat as a flapjack, relying on its natural camouflage—light, irregular spots against an earth-tone pelage—and its near (not total) lack of odor for anonymity in the midst of prowling predators. And for the most part, the hider strategy works. So long as an approaching threat is moving, instinct keeps the calf catatonic and, usually, all is well. But if the predator stops for too long too nearby—you may have witnessed this for yourself, as I have, if you've ever stumbled upon an infant elk calf or fawn—the babe may become confused and raise its naive little noggin for a peek; even try to stand and run. In which event ... *Gotcha!*

I'm reminded of a vintage anecdote related by one A. B. Howell in the "General Notes" (which could just as well be called the "Weird Wildlife Happenings") section of an antique edition of the venerable *Journal of Mammalogy*:

> On June 12, 1920, while approaching a camping site on the Lamar River, Yellowstone National Park ... I noted a black bear hunting around through the sage brush on a nearby hillside. Five minutes later ... I turned my ten power glasses on the bear, and was surprised to see that he was making off, at a leisurely gait, with an elk calf in his mouth. He paid not the slightest attention to the presumable mother of the calf, which followed him anxiously within fifteen or twenty feet.

That calf had likely moved at just the wrong time, and consequently, for the last time—exactly as I've seen happen my ownself, also on the Lamar River in Yellowstone, but with grizzlies, wolves and coyotes as the "bad guys."

A more recent example of how the hider strategy does and sometimes doesn't work occurred a few years ago just up the mountain from my shack. At the time, the third member of our little family was a big black-and-gold retriever-setter mix of calm disposition. Over the years, Caroline and I had trained Amigo not to chase the wildlife that occasionally breaks and flees close ahead during our long evening walks in the neighboring woods; with good old Amigo, it hadn't been hard.

But all of that changed one June evening when a sleek cow elk stepped boldly from a trailside oak-brush patch and into the open just a few yards ahead—and stood there and stared. Considering the season and previous experiences with this sort of thing, I suspected immediately what was up. Taking our cue from the cow, Caroline and I just stood and traded stares with the big mother, not noticing that Amigo had slipped off and was nosing around in the brush from which the cow had materialized.

At first, the old hound couldn't seem to locate the little hider he obviously suspected was lurking there, but he must have been getting warm because suddenly the cow lost her cool and barked. At this alarming signal the calf jumped up and ran for its mother—and smack into Amigo, who stood fortuitously between. Ignoring our shouted commands to the contrary, Amigo, acting on some dim wolfish imperative, tackled the calf and knocked it to the ground. And there they lay, the calf outwardly calm (the silence of the lamb), awaiting its fate, while Amigo looked at us and grinned, his tongue lolling happily, standing astraddle the floored calf but otherwise doing it no harm.

I sprinted up, grabbed Amigo by the scruff and jerked him clear of the calf—at which happy turn the infant bull wobbled to his feet and scampered to his anxious mother's side. The last we saw of them, they were trotting (not running) away with nary a glance back, apparently no worse for the wear and likely a wee bit the wiser.

In this encounter, it was the mother, not the calf, who'd buckled beneath the prolonged pressure and blown the game. Still, the fact that the hider strategy could fail to the extent of allowing a sick old house pet (Amigo would die of cancer just two weeks later) to make such an easy "virtual" kill suggests that it fails with great regularity in the face of practiced wild predators. It's almost as if evolution, in shaping such an imperfect defense, intended that a tithe of cervid young become protein for hungry carnivores—who, after all, have their own young to feed. Just so.

☙

The classic scientific study of elk calf predation by black bears was monitored and reported by Idaho Regional Wildlife Manager Mike Schlegel, stretching across three summers in the mid-1970s. The study area comprised about eighty square miles of north-central Idaho's Clearwater region. An abstract snatched from *Elk of North America* offers an overview:

> [This study] followed the fortunes of fifty-three [elk] calves that survived capture and radio-collaring within a few days of birth. Of these, six appeared to have been killed by mountain lions and twenty-eight by black bears within the first few weeks of life.

Those alarmingly high stats—twenty-eight of fifty-three calves killed and eaten by bears—could lead one to worry that bears inflict an equally damaging toll on elk calves throughout the two species' extensive overlapping ranges.

Not so. Bear density in the Clearwater region during the three years of the study was atypically (one might say incredibly) high—about two bruins per square mile. When averaged across its entire western North American range, black bear density is but a fraction of that. As pre-eminent grizzly researcher Charles Jonkel of Montana says in the opening sentence of his treatise in *Big Game of North America*, "bears are large, wide-ranging animals with low reproductive rates and low population densities." Beyond such ball-park ambiguities, few biologists are willing to step. But there's no argument that the Clearwater study area came equipped with an abnormally high bear population. Good luck for the researchers. Bad luck for the elk.

Why, we're left to wonder, were there so very many bears in that particular eighty-square-mile parcel at exactly elk calving season three years running? Schlegel suggests two possibilities. First, since black bears leave the winter den craving moist, green pastures—grasses, sedges, forbs and the like—it's natural they would gravitate to identical spring microhabitats that attract winter-lean elk.

Second, the same bears and bear families likely had been preying on elk calves in the Clearwater region every spring for years. Being clever creatures with good memories for an easy meal, bears learn through experience exactly where to be, and when to be there, in order to enjoy the brief elk hunting season nature grants them. It's a situation not unlike Alaskan brown bears congregating along certain stretches of certain streams to gorge on spawning salmon—same bears, same stream, same time of year, year after year.

But natural influences are hardly the only influences at work here. In a phone conversation, Schlegel suggested to me a surprising additional variable likely affecting the size of localized bear populations—and, consequently, predation rates—most anywhere. That variable is bear hunting.

Since big, mature bears—dominant males in particular—establish and defend fairly large territories, you'll find lower bear densities in areas enjoying balanced bruin populations including sufficient mature animals. Conversely, smaller bears—especially females, with or without cubs, and subadult males—are more likely to (often *must*) tolerate the nearby presence of one another and learn to live within smaller territories. Thus, across a given area, the presence of older and bigger male bears suggests fewer bears total, while a younger population forecasts more animals per given block of suitable habitat; the richer the habitat, the more bears.

Thing is, your average bear hunter, like your average elk hunter, wants to bag the biggest animal he or she can find—a "trophy." (How easy to despise that despicable term!) But unlike elk hunting, most bear killing traditionally has been done with the crutches of baits and hounds. Well-placed and regularly replenished baits generally attract several bears, serially, making it relatively easy for a patient shooter to pick and choose. Similarly, a hound hunter can tree bears serially, until he finds the one he (and these days, she) wants.

Consequently, areas in which bears are regularly hunted with baits or hounds tend to have lower mature male populations (because they get selectively culled) and, consequently, higher overall bear numbers. (Unless, of course, hunting pressure is so intense as to eliminate most *all* the bears, no matter big or small, which happened a lot in the past, but rarely today.) Since a small bear can kill an elk calf just as dead as can a large bear, two small bears can kill twice as many calves as one large bear and the potential for calf predation is doubled.

Schlegel's research confirms that in elk calving areas where black bear numbers are exceptionally high, spring predation can be a significant factor—perhaps *the* significant factor—in infant elk mortality. Yet, and seemingly contrary to logic, the total number of calves in an area appears to have little bearing on the number killed.

Why so?

So, because of the limited hunting season during which bears are effective predators on elk calves. Schlegel found that 84 percent of *all* (not just bear) predation on elk calves during the three years of the Idaho study occurred prior to June 15, by which time most calves were strong enough to run with a protective nursery herd. This being the case, Schlegel explains, "it is possible for predators to capture only a limited number of calves by mid-June," no matter the number available to them. The term for this cervid-saving phenomenon is "predator swamping."

Put graphically, whether there are one hundred calves or five hundred, X number of predators working among them are going to have time and appetite enough to catch and eat only Y number of infants during a brief feeding frenzy, mid-May through early June.

Yet, even though the number of elk calves in an area appears to have little bearing on the number lost to predators, it has great bearing on what a given predation loss bodes for herd health a few years down the line. If, let's say, fifty calves are nabbed by predators from a total of five hundred, that's a 10 percent loss. No sweat in the big picture. But if that same fifty calves are lost from only a hundred born, the predation rate leaps to a staggering 50 percent. This loss, in turn, would of course mean a smaller breeding population in coming years, resulting in even fewer calves, a yet-higher relative predation loss (assuming the number of predators remains constant) — and so on in a downward spiral toward local extirpation.

In former, more natural times, such bottlenecks sorted themselves out over the long haul. But today, the way we've got nature all chopped up and tied down, it might occasionally be necessary to reduce unnaturally high predator numbers on the calving grounds of dangerously small elk herds; during the Idaho study, to continue the example at hand, seventy-five bears were trapped and relocated in an effort to improve cow-calf ratios. It worked, sort of, but habitat deficiencies were also helping to hold the Clearwater elk population down, and removing predators doesn't improve habitat one whit. And too, when the old bears were removed, new bears promptly arrived to fill the vacuum (that state which nature so abhors).

All points tallied, the best long-term defense against harmful levels of elk predation is not predator control, but assuring large, properly age- and gender-balanced elk herds with plenty of prime habitat across which to scatter, most particularly in winter. Always, that's the bottom line for wapiti—habitat. Quick fixes such as pogromatic predator control rarely fix anything.

Which brings us to the core of this drunken inquiry: Can bear predation have a worrisome negative impact on elk populations? Or not?

Not likely.

Remember, first of all, that even though bears are classed scientifically under the order Carnivora, they are not hard-core carnivores—like, say, cougars and wolves—but opportunistic omnivores, like humans. Both black and grizzly bears are overwhelmingly vegetarian, to the tune, more or less, of 90 percent.

Remember too that beyond the brief weeks of calving season when the livin' and dyin' is easy, bears, especially black bears, are pretty poor predators, almost never catching and pulling down healthy animals, nor even often trying to. This is due in great part to timing: During winter when even big bulls can be relatively easy for mega-predators to run down and worry to death in deep snow, bears are snoozing dreamily in den.

In the long view (the only view that counts), the only elk predators effective enough to be truly damaging are—humans: hunters, ranchers, loggers, subdividers, you and me, intentionally and otherwise. And of that motley lot, the only ones who are monitored, controlled, even manipulated to help achieve beneficent wildlife ends, are hunters.

The buck stops here: North America has an abundance of elk and no glut of bears or other natural predators. In other words, regarding bear predation on elk: it is not to worry. To the contrary, the question isn't whether or not bears kill elk—sure they do—it is whether bears kill *enough* elk to keep the herds culled of genetic marginalia (which, like it or not, Bambis always are) and trimmed to the capacity of their habitat. If we can just maintain the habitat, nature will tend to the rest.

Delighted with my scatological detective work, I clean the tiny hoof shells as best I can, wrap them in a skunk-cabbage leaf and stow them in my pack. At my house, to my wife, they and the story they tell, the wild mystery they evoke, will be as warmly received as a big old bunch of roses.

Griz the Elk Hunter

AFTER MAN AND WOLF, the grizzly bear is the wapiti's tertiary external predator. It's fair to say, I believe, that no matter how many elk grizzlies manage to catch and devour—or scavenge as carrion—they never grow tired of eating wapiti ... or deer, or marmots, or much of any other meaty manna. When John Muir allowed as how the grizzly will swallow anything but granite, he understated; I've found marble-sized metamorphic pebbles in bear scat many's the time.

With bears, black as well as "white" (as Lewis and Clark and other early explorers often called grizzlies), it's not preference so much as opportunity. Throughout their seven or so waking months each year, grizzlies back-hoe for rodents, slap shallow water for fish and snatch larger prey as opportunity allows. Even so, as a backdrop and safety net, the plants are *always* there, providing reliable, easy pickings that don't hide, run away or fight back, and which, therefore, account for most of the grizzly's groceries.

So important are greens to bears that if you know what vegetal foods are available and prime where and when, you've got a leg up on locating your grizzer. By and large, in early spring you're likely to spot grizzlies—fresh from den and hungry as teenage boys—digging for tubers and grazing on fresh sprouts in sunny subalpine meadows where the snow has gone out early. A little later in the season, drifting (like elk) ever higher, they'll be working shaded alpine slopes and avalanche chutes where green-up is delayed by lingering snow. In late summer and fall, berries and mast—especially squirrel-cached nuts—bring bears back down the mountain and dominate their predenning diet.

Of the minority flesh portion of the grizzly's fare, it's generally not fresh-killed game, but insects and carrion that make up the bulk. All considered, the odds are overwhelming in favor of finding a grizzly nipping wildflowers, knocking apart a rotten log looking for insects or gnawing on winterkill rather than drinking the blood of an elk or other large mammal it has slain.

Of course, grizzlies do eat fresh-killed meat, including especially elk, when they can get it. When the resource is rich and an opportunity presents itself, or can be created, some grizzlies—having learned the profitability of concerted predation from their mothers, or by observing other bears hunting, or through fortuitous happenstance—become fearsome and skilled elk hunters. They search, they stalk, they chase, they ambush, they—like the more competent among their human counterparts—*plan* their hunts.

If you don't care for, can't accept or abide by such rash anthropomorphic statements as that last—the proposition that grizzlies have the intelligence to plan ahead—I invite you to visit Yellowstone National Park next spring. There, in late May and early June, if you care to wait and watch, you can witness grizzlies employing not only thoughtful, but spontaneously adaptive tactics to hunt newborn elk calves.

Early in the spring calving season, the most common and productive hunting strategy employed by grizzlies is the slow search; in one study (French and French, 1988) searching for hiding calves accounted for 75 percent of sixty grizzly elk hunts observed. After spotting an alert lone cow elk, or often a pair of cows—which, it appears, suggests to savvy grizzlies (as it does to me) the likelihood of a calf hiding nearby—the bear may charge and chase the cow or cows away, then methodically criss-cross the area, looking low and high, sniffing and occasionally stopping, standing motionless, ears alert for the subtlest sound of movement or vocalization made by the wee hidden meal. I myself have watched mother grizz (the plural of griz) with subadult cubs working as a team, "fanning out" to skillfully scour an aspen grove, sage flat or other likely calving ground. The effort is worth it, with nearly half of all observed slow searches ending with the hunter dining on elk veal.

Of course, almost any large predator can kill infant calves, with coyotes, cougars, black bears and wolves all getting in on the meaty action. The tricky bit is *finding* the little imps. And in this endeavor, grizzlies aren't just any predators.

❦

It was early spring, and Doug Peacock was out doing his thing— the thing he's become famous for with his award-winning PBS documentary "Peacock's War" and his instant-classic book *Grizzly Years*—that is, bear watching. Not an academic biologist and proud of it, Peacock nonetheless is widely considered a leading authority on the behavior of grizzlies in the wild.

This particular early spring morn, Doug was camped in a backcountry area of the Firehole region of Yellowstone Park. The snow was mostly gone from the open thermal flats, but still lay deep along the shaded meadow edges and back beneath the trees. Elk and bison still were bunched in big winter herds, and when a grizzly boar—"a big, black, untagged, anonymous bear"—exploded out of the lodgepoles to bust up a covey of wapiti that had wandered near the timber where the hunter had been waiting in ambush, Peacock was there to watch. As he recalls the episode:

"At first it didn't look like much would happen. The elk just loped away, with the grizzly loping along after them. But then the bear picked up on something about one of the cows—old age, infirmity, something invisible to me but clearly apparent to the grizzly—and in an instant things got serious. The bear put on a tremendous burst of speed and within another hundred feet caught up with the cow, rearing up on his hind legs and slamming his front paws down on her back, collapsing her hips with his weight."

When the cow went down, Peacock made a dash back into the timber, where he was bivouacked, to fetch his camera. When he returned, less than a minute later, the bear was shaking the elk "like a cat with a mouse." When the hunter was sure the cow was good and dead, he eviscerated the carcass with a couple of swipes of claw and dragged his prize back into the timber to feed.

"I'd been tracking this bear every day," Peacock recounts, "so I knew a bit about him even though I got to see him only twice; he was very secretive. But he was bedding in the same relatively small stand of timber where I was camped, and I was finding his kills everywhere. It looked like he was taking an elk maybe a couple of times a week. He didn't even eat the entire carcasses. He'd chew on 'em until he got his fill, then abandon the kill; he didn't always even bother to cover them with debris. But nothing went to waste. As soon as the bear was gone, the coyotes and ravens showed up to finish the job. That griz was feeding a lot of wildlife besides himself that spring."

Nor was this a freak occurrence. Again, Doug Peacock:

"Old Number Fifteen was the bear that went nuts after being trapped and drugged too many times; finally had to be executed after killing a camper at Rainbow Point. But for years, Number Fifteen was a superb elk hunter, taking mature, healthy animals spring through fall, including prime bulls. He was the best elk-killing bear I've ever known, especially during the rut. In fact, second only to early spring, when the wapiti are still herded up and winter-weak and there's snow still on the ground to slow their escape, the rut is the most opportune time for grizzlies to take mature bulls, since dominant male elk are love-struck and let their defenses down.

"Certain springs—1969 was one—you see all kinds of predation on adult elk by grizzlies, especially in Gardiner Hole and along the Firehole River. I remember one subadult bear who, after chasing down and killing an elk, would almost always get run off by a bigger grizzly—so he'd have to turn around and go after another elk. Tourists were just hanging around and watching this happening."

Hearing such stories, it's tempting to hop to the conclusion that grizzlies are devastating predators on elk. But remember, these events took and take place in and adjacent to Yellowstone Park, a proudly protected, densely concentrated ecosystem where at least three hundred grizzlies roam and elk are beyond abundant, their self-endangering surplus begging to be trimmed.

(I'm reminded here of a cartoon: Two buck deer are watching a hunter in the distance, and one buck remarks to the other, "Why don't they have hunting seasons to control their *own* population?" I didn't view the 'toon as an antihunting barb, but as a cogent comment on our dualistic, anthropocentric approach to "wildlife" management, when in fact it is ourselves, our own bloated and sloppy-minded population, that's in greatest need of managing and curtailing.)

Back in 1972, Glen Cole, of the National Park Service's Office of Natural Science Studies, published a paper titled "Grizzly Bear – Elk Relationships in Yellowstone National Park," summarizing studies that began in 1967 and continued through 1971. Cole's seminal study suggests that while grizzly predation alone isn't essential to maintaining a healthy wapiti herd in the park, it's nonetheless an essential part of a coalition of natural forces working together to moderate potentially catastrophic boom-and-crash cycles in wapiti numbers. Culling. Pruning. Survival of those most suited to survive and reproduce. Natural selection in action.

While there are of course exceptions, bears and other predators attempt to maximize calories gained in hunting compared to calories expended. (Otherwise, why bother?) To do so, they ferret out the most easily catchable meals—the young, the old, the sick, lame, lazy, stupid and momentarily disadvantaged. Pursuing this patient pace, the prey population is continually skimmed of its marginalia, assuring that all available food resources, often critically short in winter, go to those elk best qualified not just to survive, but to successfully rear healthy offspring. Biologists see this direct sort of natural selection at work in calf predation, in that the "wisest" and, therefore, fittest cows choose the best hiding places for their young and otherwise defend them most effectively against predation, thus giving their calves a survival advantage over the offspring of meeker or less clever or less experienced or otherwise less fit cows.

In sum, Yellowstone's grizzlies were determined by the Cole study to contribute to the *quality* of the elk herd, even as they carved only a slight reduction in elk quantity.

Nor has anything changed. Today's bear biologists hold Cole's 1970s observations and conclusions as still valid: Grizzlies still prey on both calves and mature elk, as opportunity arises, but this predation has only an "adjunct" influence on overall elk mortality and is both natural and positive in the long haul.

Kerry Gunther, who runs the Yellowstone Bear Management Office, conducted a somewhat more recent grizzly predation study (1984–88) in the Pelican Valley area. Gunther offers his conclusions in the paper "Grizzly Bear Predation on Elk Calves and other Fauna of Yellowstone National Park," suggesting that grizzly predation on elk calves has increased since Cole's day. But, as Gunther recently assured me, this is hardly a bad sign:

"Back when the park policy was to thin the elk herds [by transplanting and shooting] in order to keep their numbers down to around five thousand on the northern range, there were fewer calves for predators to hunt, and therefore less opportunity for bears to learn how to hunt them successfully. Now, with the Northern herd alone numbering in excess of twenty thousand elk, predation naturally is up."

As well it should be.

"As far back as the park has kept records, bears have preyed on elk calves. But the window of opportunity for catching calves is so short—mid-May through mid-June—that the number lost to predators is insignificant when compared to, say, the number of adult elk that wander outside the park and are taken by hunters."

And cars and dogs and ...

When I asked Gunther about the level of grizzly predation on adult elk in the park today, I was little surprised when his official opinion corroborated Doug Peacock's anecdotal reports. "Carcass surveys," he told me, "suggest a certain amount of bear predation on winter-weakened adult elk during early spring, though we can't say exactly how much because that sort of activity is so rarely observed. There's also evidence of grizzlies taking a few bulls in the fall, during the rut.

"Predation," Kerry Gunther concluded, "is a natural and positive influence on elk, which in no way regulates populations; the primary elk population regulators are hunting and the availability of winter range."

True enough for the special case of Yellowstone. But what about elsewhere—like, say, farther north, up along northern Montana's Front Range, where hundreds of grizzlies and thousands of elk coexist, not crammed together as in Yellowstone, but scattered across a much broader, far more remote and less peopled expanse of wilderness?

🌿

Michael Madel, a grizzly biologist for the Montana Department of Fish, Wildlife and Parks (FWP), is saddled with the awesome responsibility of monitoring the grizzly population and minimizing bear/human conflicts along much of the length of the Rocky Mountain Front on the eastern slope of the sprawling Northern Continental Divide Ecosystem (NCDE). Madel's beat includes the Great Bear and Scapegoat wilderness areas, plus a portion of the huge Bob Marshall—"the Bob," as it's locally known. I asked Madel about grizzly predation there.

"From research we've conducted, we're confident that grizzly predation has little effect on the elk population. We just don't see the concerted predatory behavior they regularly observe down in Yellowstone. Except for the North and West forks of the Sun River, there just aren't all that many elk-calving grounds up here that are readily available to grizzlies—except on the preserve; that's a different story."

Madel is referring to the state-owned Sun River Game Preserve, where some three thousand elk spend their springs and summers and human predation is not permitted. In effect, it's a mini-Yellowstone minus the tourists and thermal features. The lower, eastern stretch of the preserve even topographically resembles the fecund Lamar Valley calving grounds of Yellowstone Park. And, as at Yellowstone, local grizzlies have discovered that elk hunting pays.

Before taking a "cushy indoor job" as the preserve's laboratory manager, grizzly biologist Keith Aune enjoyed a long and distinguished career studying bears throughout the Northern Continental Divide Ecosystem.

"The Sun River Game Preserve provides elk with an excellent calving area," Aune told me. "Consequently, we see a fair bit of grizzly predation on elk calves here. The tendency has been to consider it incidental, but my gut feeling is that what we're seeing is just the tip of an iceberg; there's probably a lot more elk calf predation going on than our studies have picked up. Sun River has traditionally not had a a great cow-calf ratio. It's not impossible—when you consider grizzlies, black bears, coyotes and the other carnivores here—that predation could be a contributing factor."

I asked Aune if he felt that grizzly predation across the NCDE cut into elk numbers to the point it could make a difference in the success rates of hunters—who, after all, make up the primary life-support system for elk and most other wildlife. I admit to being a bit surprised by his affirmative answer. Even so, Aune's confirmation of the recurring "quality over quantity" theme is reassuring:

"Certainly, it's possible that predation could have a little influence on hunter success; I wouldn't say it has *no* influence. But I would argue that in terms of the overall health of the herd and the ecosystem, predators balance out as a benefit to elk management rather than a detriment. For one thing, predators are better selectors of prey fitness than are human hunters; predators help to hone the genetic fitness of the herd by selecting for [that is, rewarding] physical health and superior defensive behavior patterns."

The Northern Continental Divide Ecosystem is a long, narrow chain of designated wilderness areas comprising approximately six million acres total, stretching from Glacier National Park on the north down the Whitefish and Flathead ranges as far south as Rogers Pass and Montana Highway 200. How many grizzlies, I asked Aune, might it sustain?

"We figure 490 to 690, with densities varying from one bear per fifty square miles, up to one per ten square miles. But interestingly, the general distribution of grizzlies appears to be just about reverse that of elk, with more bears in marginal elk habitat and fewer bears in strong elk habitat."

Finally, I asked Keith about the hunting methods most commonly employed by Sun River grizzlies.

"Through radiotelemetry and snow-tracking, we know that grizzlies up here—just like those down in Yellowstone—use a variety of tactics, especially ambush and stalking. One common ploy is for a bear to use natural cover to stalk close to a group of elk, then run toward them, testing, trying to identify an animal that appears vulnerable."

Peacock *redux*.

"We've also seen strong indications of ambush. I found one place, for instance, where bones and other evidence suggested that a grizzly had been regularly 'setting up' there to ambush calves. It was in a jungly bottom where elk were likely to be feeding around the abundant edge cover; the bear, it appeared, would lie in ambush and jump any calf that fed past.

"A third common technique used by grizzlies to hunt elk is searching out the hiding places of newborn calves [the aforementioned "slow search"]. Experienced grizzlies seem to know just by looking at a cow whether or not she has a calf hidden nearby. In fact, this search strategy is probably the most effective for *all* predators of elk—grizzlies, black bears, wolves, lions and probably even coyotes. Collectively, this could add up to a significant impact.

"Of course, how you interpret the 'significance' of predation depends on your frame of reference. If you're an elk manager trying to maximize herd numbers, predation can become an important factor. But if you're looking at it from a broader ecological perspective, predation by no means controls elk populations. And in the long view, one important natural role elk play is to help sustain predators for a healthy ecosystem.

"For example, during hunting season, bears seem to be coming down the Sun River looking for wounded and dead elk that have fled onto the preserve—cleaning up man's mistakes. And there are other interesting interactions between elk, bears and human hunters as well. A lot of hunters are reporting that bugling for elk sometimes attracts grizzlies. As a bowhunter, I've personally experienced cases of grizzlies checking out hunting camps and searching hunting areas for gutpiles and meat left in the field overnight. And you can have situations where a hunter and a bear are trailing the same wounded animal. All of this, of course, is evidence of bears learning new behavior patterns that will put meat in their stomachs."

The elements of elk predation by grizzlies I personally find most intriguing are the bruins' strikingly manlike hunting tactics: the slow search, stalking, driving (where one bear/hunter waits in a blocking position while another bear/hunter pushes, or drives, the prey out of hiding and toward his waiting partner), ambushing and more. I'd heard tell that Jamie Jonkel (son of famed grizzly biologist Charles Jonkel) was a walking warehouse of grizzly-elk predation stories, so I gave him a call.

Jonkel works today up along the North Fork of the Flathead River with the godfather of mountain lion researchers, Maurice Hornocker (who, in turn, got his start back in the 1950s studying Yellowstone/Teton grizzlies with the renowned Craighead brothers). Along the way, Jonkel spent years tramping the Yellowstone backcountry collecting data on bears for noted grizzly biologist Dick Knight of the Interagency Grizzly Bear Study Team. Tallying his own observations with those of his fellow researchers, Jonkel is in fact a walking wealth of grizzly elk-hunting lore. Like, for instance, his account of a grizzly killing a mature bull:

"While working for Dick Knight, field biologist Bart Schleyer [since deceased] and some companions made camp in the West Yellowstone area early one spring following a heavy snow winter. From there, they ranged out to survey grizzly activity. One radio-collared sow, Number Thirty-eight, had a couple of cubs that year and Bart's crew went out one evening to track her. As they homed toward the radio signal, they heard all kinds of crashing around, out of sight, across a small draw. Then came the death scream of an elk."

The researchers, being neither greenhorns nor fools, wisely retreated.

"Next morning," Jonkel continued, "they went back and found where the bear had chased a winter-weakened raghorn [a three- or four-point bull] off an open flat and up a hill into the timber. There, the bear made the kill—which the researchers had heard the final moments of the previous evening—then fed on the carcass during the night.

"In another incident, this time involving a big male grizzly, Number Fifty-one, Schleyer and some companions found where the bear had killed and fed on several adult elk. He had a regular bushwhack site where a series of major game trails wound down through some rocks to meet in the bottom of a draw. The number of bones there indicated he'd been successfully using this ambuscade for quite some time.

"A third elk-hunting bear was Number Fifty, a female living in a remote part of the West Yellowstone area, up in the rhyolite plateaus—pretty poor bear habitat so far as vegetal foods are concerned. Consequently, she had become very predacious. I recall two of her kills, both bulls. Again, it was Bart Schleyer who went into Number Fifty's area, because radio signals were indicating that she'd dropped her collar. As Bart and his companions approached, they spotted a big pile of duff with the tips of antlers sticking out. The physical evidence told of a tremendous fight: a hundred-square-yard area of earth had been churned up and the trees all around were splattered and smeared with blood. Possibly it was one of those extremely stupid rutting bulls that will sometimes stand and challenge an approaching bear. When a grizzly takes on a mature bull, it will often get right up in the antlers, hang on and beat the prey around its neck."

The bear had fed, then covered the carcass with duff. Since only about a third of the kill had been consumed, it was likely that Number Fifty was still in the area; again, the researchers wisely retreated.

In the "believe it or not" category is a story that came to Jonkel through a fellow biologist, who in turn mined it from a 1920s Norwegian sporting magazine. "Some fellow," Jamie summarized, "heard the ["roaring"] calls of what he thought was a red deer in rut. Working his way toward the sounds, he spotted a brown [grizzly] bear making strange squeals and growls, apparently trying to 'bugle in' a rutting bull!"

True or false, it's a killer story, eerily reminiscent of another such tale, this one undoubtedly true, as recorded by Russian explorer Vladimir Arseniev, the one-man Siberian Lewis and Clark, in his book *Dersu the Trapper*. It was early September, 1907, and the captain and his Manchurian aboriginal guide, Dersu Uzala, were out one evening hunting wapiti to feed their hungry camp. As an animist—the universal, beautifully reciprocal hunter-gatherer worldview—Dersu saw all living things as equals, a belief he expressed by referring to animals (in his quaint pidgin Russian) as "men." Of the tiger incident, Arseniev writes:

> Suddenly Dersu stopped and listened. He turned round and stood motionless. There came to my ear the roar of an old stag, but the note was somewhat different.
> "Hm," muttered Dersu. "Understand what man him?"
> I replied that I supposed it was a wapiti, an old one.
> "Him Amba!" he whispered to me. "Him very clever man. Him all time trap wapiti like that. Wapiti now not understand, not know what man call. Amba soon catch hind."

And as in confirmation of his words, at that moment the deep voice of a stag answered the tiger, which at once replied. He made a very fair imitation of the roar of the stag, but at the end broke off in a sort of deep purr. The great cat was coming nearer, and would soon probably pass quite close to us.

Incredible, yes. But hardly in-credible. Arseniev was a no-nonsense military man and reliable natural historian. The "wapiti" in question is the small-antlered Manchurian model, or Izbur stag, in fact a red deer (*C. e. xanthopygus*). Its rutting call is described by Arseniev as "belling, grunting and roaring," rather than the long-drawn, high brassy bugle of a true wapati. I find it wholly believable that a talented tiger could ape the Izbur stag's rutting call well enough to dupe a testosterone-poisoned bull.

And too, my optimism in this matter is based in part on my brief tenure as a sub-minimum-wage slave at a private Montana zoo, where I labored butchering foundered livestock and road-killed deer to toss to the toothy menagerie of carnivores imprisoned there, including a brace of Bengal tigers. Having heard the versatile vocalizations of tigers up close, I buy easily into the Dersu story.

For the heck of it, I ran the tiger anecdote past Valerius Geist, an expert on Siberian as well as North American ungulates. He responded that "the tiger luring red deer with its call is new to me, though the similarity between the territorial call of the tiger and of the rutting red deer is not." Like me, Geist has no trouble swallowing Arseniev's tale, adding this sad postscript: "Today, there are very few Siberian tigers left. Once, they roamed right into the heart of Alaska, along with true lions."

A Pleistocene paradise lost.

❧

Shifting our conversation to grizzly predation on elk calves, Jonkel offered that "probably the most common technique—after the slow search for hiders—is for a bear to charge into a nursery herd of cows and calves, trying to separate the little ones from their mothers, knocking down as many as possible before going back along the line to eat, peeling the calves like bananas and scarfing them down essentially whole; all that's left is a rolled-up wad of hide, hooves and a few bones. No waste."

This run-and-scatter caper is most common in late June, when the calves have matured sufficiently to come out of hiding and travel with the herd.

"So yes," Jonkel concluded, "grizzlies prey on elk, especially in Yellowstone. But elk are thick there—they're *everywhere*. It's like the hubbub about 'all the deer' killed by wolves in other areas. Compared to the number of deer killed by hunters and automobiles, the natural predation loss is piddling. Up in the Swan Valley, above Missoula, it's not uncommon to see as many as eight deer a day killed on local highways."

As an indicator species teetering at the top of a dynamic food chain, grizzlies are like the miner's canary in that their health, or lack thereof, serves as an indicator of the health, or lack thereof, of the entire ecosystem, elk especially included.

Bear experts in Yellowstone country and elsewhere report that grizzly populations have been enjoying a "positive trend" in the past few years, with lower female mortality and a higher cub birth and survival rate. Nonetheless, ongoing poaching, preventable "accidents" (such as the infamous case where several bears were splattered by speeding trains as they fed on fermented grain spilled onto the tracks by passing boxcars and not cleaned up), losses of bears and bear habitat to the insatiable livestock and logging industries and to commercial and residential development, all bode ill for the grizzly's future in the lower forty-eight.

At best, the great bear's population is hardly "bulging at the seams," as a certain self-important hook-and-bullet hack proclaims. To the contrary, as Doug Peacock has pointed out in *Audubon* and elsewhere, Yellowstone grizzlies are being forced to wander *because they are starving*.

Rather than "bulging at the seams," the seams are rapidly tightening, closing in on what precious few American grizzlies remain ... closing in on elk and other wildlife that share the grizzly's habitat ... closing in on all things wild and free, including you, including me.

In Defense of
Predators

We are kindred all of us, killer and victim, predator and prey.
—Edward Abbey

I'M SITTING AT MY plywood-plank desk, out in the Outhouse, doing what I call work, when my blushing bride comes slumping in, brown eyes tearing. I ask what's wrong.

"A raven just took a robin chick from the nest down by my garden. I yelled at it and threw rocks, but it ignored me. It just breaks my heart to see that kind of thing."

Of course it does, notwithstanding that the raven in question, a local bird, has nestlings of her own to feed and robin chicks are in good supply this spring.

This is life. Which is to say: *death* is life.

Not long before his own death at the wizened age of ninety, I received a letter from A. B. "Bud" Guthrie, Jr., Montana's grand old man of literature and my self-appointed "writing coach" (his term, my honor). It was winter and Bud had just watched a weasel chase down and kill a rabbit. "I tried like hell to be objective," he wrote, "knowing weasels have to earn a living the only way they can. Yet my sentiments stayed with the rabbit. Why do you suppose that is?"

Good question.

But for whatever reasons, even rural folk like Bud Guthrie and my Caroline tend to side with the prey, the underdogs. Nor am I immune to prey-sympathy, finding it, for example, deeply disturbing to watch live lobsters scuttling about in a supermarket tank, their claws bound with rubber bands, their once-oceanic world reduced to a few murky gallons of water, their destiny to be tossed, some say screaming, into a pot of boiling water. And who is the predator here?

Most people today, in particular those who live in cities and have few opportunities to witness wild nature in action, seem to harbor at least an innate suspicion of all predators, including especially the blaze-orange human form.

Odd, this, given that humans have been hunters since before we were human. And for all but the last ten millennia or so of our multi-million-year run as *Homo*, hunting and gathering were *all* we did. Hunting filled our days with challenge and action, our nights with story. Hunting inspired our dreams and art and myths and religions, helping significantly to shape what we are today, for better and for worse.

Somewhere within this perplexing tug-o'-war lurks the answer to Bud Guthrie's Gordian query: Given a generically embedded prey-sympathy pulling at our civilization-refined emotions from one side, even as generic memories from our bottomless hunting history tug from the other, it's small wonder that people's feelings today about predation and hunting are so strong, so confusing and ultimately so divisive. The human animal, as evolutionary philosopher Paul Shepard so eloquently pointed out, is the oxymoronic "tender carnivore."

Hunting is one of the hardest things even to think about. Such a storm of conflicting emotions! Indeed, Cactus Ed, it is.

Taking prey-sympathy and its implied mortality-denial to the extreme, the more simplistic and sentimental among us imagine that *all* predation is evil and that all predators, human and non, are cruel—the Big Bad Wolves of nursery rhyme infamy. Animal rights guru Cleveland Amory and like-minded others have gone so far as to suggest that it would be good to eliminate not only hunting, but natural predation as well. In such a Bambified perfect world, wolves would literally lie down with caribou calves (let 'em eat grass!), wildlife populations no longer self-regulating via Tennyson's law of "nature red in tooth and claw," but human-controlled via ... contraceptives!

Hubris and hypocrisy. Life is no more possible without ubiquitous violent death than without oxygen or water. Nor could evolution operate; as scholar Stephen J. Gould points out, "the price of perfect design is messy, relentless slaughter."

Just so. Yet, as Paul Shepard points out, "That animals live by eating other creatures, that more than 50 percent of the newborns will not live for a year, that predators and scavengers are good and necessary—this is incompatible with the sentimental cloak that characterizes the nineteenth and twentieth century animal story, the Walt Disney view."

It's hard, but it works. The "cruel" raven who abducts the "sweet" little robin chick in order to feed her own young, the "vicious" weasel who devours the "poor" rabbit, the "monstrous" bear and the "evil" wolf who prey on the "helpless" elk calf— such anthropomorphic labeling and thinking, to which we all at one time and another are prone, assigns moral judgments where none can apply. "Cruelty" suggests a wanton or at least willful infliction of physical or mental suffering (as in industrial livestock operations and—the horror!—vivisection), and thus is a glaring non sequitur when applied to nature, which wills nothing, but simply *is*.

Natural predation is neither moral, immoral nor even amoral, but beyond all such human-constructed bounds. It is not a freely chosen—Sartre's "for itself"—"lifestyle" to be measured in human terms, but the wild carnivore's *only means of living*—

Sartre's "in itself"—necessitated by that most basic of biological imperatives: gut-burning hunger. The goal of a ravished wolf is to get meat on the ground and into its stomach before a bigger, badder predator comes along to take it away. If the elk calf is not entirely dead before it goes down the gullet, it's no fault of the wolf's, who did not design the system.

What weapons has the lion but himself? eh, Mr. Keats?

Human hunters, of which I am a picky but passionate one, being predators ourselves, should understand this intricate and essential predator-prey relationship better than most. Yet, many within hunting's raggedy ranks are among the worst of predator-phobics (surpassed only by the livestock industry and their political and bureaucratic Department of Agriculture sycophants), waging war ruthlessly, self-righteously, even gleefully against nonhuman carnivores, whom they greedily view as competitors. Sadly and traditionally, such arrogant actions and attitudes have been endorsed by much of the rest of the so-called hunting fraternity, if not explicitly, at least implicitly via apathetic or fearful silence.

I am here to challenge that gutless paradigm.

Through four decades of intimately personal experience, I've evolved an unshakable belief that the essence—and thus the moral justification and greatest reward—of so-called "sport" hunting lies in challenge, in woodcraft, in humility, in respect (if not love) for the animals we hunt and the country we hunt them in, evidenced by an eager willingness to protect and propagate both.

A note on terminology: The word "sport" was first applied to "blood sport" more than a century ago in an attempt to distinguish hunting and fishing for meat and recreation—at that time almost universally considered wholesome—from market hunting and commercial fishing ... *not* to suggest a parallel between field and stream sports—which most often are quiet, individual undertakings that play out in private—and the macho-mania of spectator sports. Nevertheless, just such a negative association has evolved, at least in the minds of antihunters who bend it to their will. Don't believe it.

As a traditional—that is, voluntarily low-tech—bowhunter, I strive to emulate natural predators, relying on skill, patience and an intricate, intimate knowledge of my prey's habits and haunts in order to get close enough to make meat. And like the cougar, the bear, the fox and other natural-born hunters, I fail far more often than I succeed.

Which is exactly as it should and must be.

From this long-standing hunter's kinship with the natural world, I've gained a strong affection and respect for predators as well as prey, and am shamed and angered by such transparently self-serving hunters' rationalizations as "the more game we let predators kill, the less there'll be for us." Such intellectually adolescent sentiments, voiced by killers who imagine themselves hunters, are echoed with zeal in a pitiful plethora of blatantly commercial, bottom-feeding, advertiser-sucking hook-and-bullet rags, whose hapless editors are prodded from behind by corporate greed machines.

Worse yet, such ignorance-based anti-predator attitudes, expressed in the worst of the outdoor media, often are codified in the policies and laws of state wildlife agencies—with plenty of push from state departments of agriculture, wildlife "citizen advisory boards" heavily weighted with ranchers and state legislators with personal agricultural interests and constituencies.

Take, for a recently infamous example of the "world was made for Man" dualistic attitude so prevalent among the lowest cut of hunters and those who feed on them, the Alaska Department of

Fish and Game's shameful campaign to exterminate three-quarters of the wolf population in the Alaska Range. The state's expressed goal was to increase the numbers of caribou and moose available to hunters. The hope and motivation was to further fatten the state's already bloated blood-sport industry. After pushing ahead in spite of vigorous popular, professional and scientific objection, Alaska's wolf pogrom was abruptly halted after news media worldwide unveiled gut-wrenching images of an Alaska wildlife officer shooting a leg-snared wolf, point-blank with a small-caliber handgun—*five times* before it died—plus a second wolf, snared but still alive (until it too was shot), which had chewed through its own leg in a stoic attempt to escape.

There are those in the elk hunting community, in *my* community, who would gladly do the same for wolves and bears and coyotes and more, all in a narcissistic, nepotistic effort to "produce" more elk for themselves—and in the case of commercial outfitters, for their wallets.

At such dark times, I am ashamed to call myself a hunter. "Good" hunters, I must believe, outnumber "bad" hunters many times over. But if so, why do the good remain largely silent, allowing the bad to continue getting their way through well-organized whining?

The best lack all conviction, while the worst are full of passionate intensity. Wouldn't you say, Mr. Yeats?

You bet, predators kill some of "our" prey ... so *what?*

❦

By now, you may be asking, honestly perplexed, why I'm such a raving predator lover. Simply put: because I so love the prey. A healthy ecosystem is indicated when a lot of big predators are actively culling the marginalia of a lot more big herbivores. That's the way, you could say, God planned it.

In point of biological fact, predators are not human hunters' enemies, but our friends, allies, even benefactors. It was predators, after all, who shaped the wapiti into one of the most sublime self-defense organisms ever to come down the evolutionary pike. And it is predators, and only predators—including especially ethical hunters—who can keep them thus.

How, I have to wonder, can hunters curse predators as "vermin" from one side of a morally bifurcate tongue, while howling from the other against the "ignorant antis who don't understand the need to manage prey for the prey's own good"?

Hubris and hypocrisy.

Paul Errington, wildlife biologist and Aldo Leopold Medal-winning author of *Predation and Life*, noted decades ago the abundance of "examples of human willingness—indeed eagerness—to destroy magnificent rarities to protect the commonplace."

Predators are always rare in relation to their prey. And the grandest among them—wolves, wolverines, big cats, bears—are the rarest of all; and this, in large part, because a relative handful of humans view them as competitors, convert them to prey and pursue them with official (if no longer societal) sanction and without moral restraint. The Big Bad Wolf may in fact live by tooth and claw and violent death, but in this human-dominated world, *he* is the ultimate victim.

What we call wilderness is both ecologically and spiritually incomplete without the full indigenous array of large predators sitting atop a sturdy food pyramid. Lacking frequent retreats into such pristine preserves of sanity—as active participant (hunter and fisher) as well as passive observer—I don't believe I'd care to continue on in this hideously transmogrified, spiritually bereft, increasingly pointless world. Wildness is the best, for me the *only* salve for the soul-sucking wounds rent by so-called progress. And without fierce creatures—bears, wolves, lions, coyotes, eagles—there can *be* no true wildness.

Nor am I alone in this nature-addiction. You need it too. We *all* need wildness in our lives, whether we realize it or not. For if we allow wild nature to die, murdered by human greed and stupidity, our humanity will die with it. And then what? It's a test, and we are failing.

"If you talk to the animals," advises Chief Dan George (not always just an actor), "they will talk with you and you will know each other."

I, for one, talk to the animals daily—wapiti and squirrels and ravens and owls and others—and they never fail to listen, never fail to reply. It is the essential conversation of a rich and happy life.

The Vertical Predator

SOME TIME BACK, I received a letter from a stranger living in a big eastern city. She began by explaining her status as a non-hunter with antihunting leanings and a deep concern for the welfare of wildlife. Apparently a literary masochist, she had read an essay I'd written in defense of ethical hunting for a general-interest magazine, and was responding with a not-so-general question. Her concern was that hunters, due to "a universal tendency" to seek out "trophy" males, exert an "unnatural and negative pressure on the genetic well-being of the various deer species." Her challenge to me was to refute that charge.

It's a fair question which—as a hunter, a student of wild nature and a conservationist—I hear with fair regularity. And often, it comes dressed as an antihunting polemic; an attack. To answer conclusively, I fear, is beyond me, a mere backwoods scribbler. Nevertheless, I have *opinions* on most everything; accordingly, I'll toss out a few morsels for mental mastication. Swallow or spit them out as your own tastes demand.

🦋

The "problem" of "unnatural selection" by hunters, it seems to me, is neither very much of a problem nor all so unnatural. Humans have *always* been hunters; it is, in fact, from an evolutionary point of view, an integral element, perhaps *the* integral element, of human nature. What could be more natural? As Paul Shepard so eloquently and convincingly traces it through a series

151

of scholarly yet passionate books, it was animals—by watching and naming them, hunting and killing them, dissecting and studying them, eating and worshiping them—who made us human. Moreover, those of us still sufficiently connected to our wild roots to feel such things, carry yet within us an instinctive aesthetic, a (you could say) mystical attraction to antlers, an affinity as old as our very genesis.

Certainly and sadly, many contemporary would-be hunters, knowing no better or giving not a hoot, embrace a wrong-headed, no-holds-barred quest to wedge their worthless names and starving adolescent egos into the "record books," into *any* record book, as often and as prominently as possible—the Grand Slam syndrome—frequently at phenomenal cost in money, honor and wildlife. These are the pathetics of blood sport. Yet, many serious, skilled and deeply ethical hunters strive to bag big bulls and bucks simply because mature male cervids are more beautiful (those antlers!), more elusive and, overall, more challenging than younger males or females. The fact that very few among this latter fraternity give a tinker's dam about record books or other forms of public "recognition," would seem to refute ego as their motivation.

Furthering this natural-born hunters' fixation on antlers is the fact that most states, in order to maintain healthy age- and gender-balanced cervid populations, have long prohibited or severely restricted the killing of females, thus abetting the innate human notion that there's something immoral, or at least "unmanly," about killing "the gentler sex." (When Texas, not long ago, put to death a confessed and convicted pick-axe double murderess, it provoked unprecedented protest. Had the killer been a man, no such ruckus would have erupted. Why?)

To recapitulate: Because mature male cervids are harder to find and tougher to bring to bag—being fewer, wiser and denizens of the remotest refugia—hunting them presents a greater challenge;

consequently, success offers a greater sense of accomplishment. Antlers—as lasting, bone-hard memories of that challenge and objects of natural art to boot—are universally cherished by hunters, albeit too often under the disagreeable term "trophies." Responding to and helping to perpetuate and expand this natural interest in big males, the editors of most hook-and-bullet magazines, and most writers who serve them (myself occasionally included), overtly and implicitly promote the "bigger is better" myth.

Nonetheless, it's my belief, based on four decades of active association with hunting, that most nimrods, while they might well *dream* of tagging a heavy-horned buck or bull, generally take the first legal animal they can get their sights on. Backing this theory is the statistical fact that the overwhelming majority of hunters manage to go their entire sporting careers without ever once bagging a "book-quality" animal. Of this norm, barring one spectacular exception, I am a fine example. After all, even a modest bull in hand makes for better eating and bragging than the most magnificent bull still out there in the bush. Those very few hunters who consistently succeed in bagging mature animals in fair chase comprise a tiny statistical anomaly. And for good reason: it's a damn hard row to hoe.

Should circumstances occasionally combine to defeat the probabilities as just laid out, which of course does happen, modern scientific game management—which in reality is *people* management—when not overwhelmed by politics and special-interest pressures, serves as a safety net. By using flexible hunting regulations to manipulate variables such as bag limits, ratios of males and females to be taken in a given season and area, and the age classes of males that can be killed, state game departments have done a phenomenal job of increasing cervid populations. Keeping those populations balanced, however, is proving a bit more challenging.

Here in Colorado, elk hunting long was managed to provide the best opportunity for the largest number of hunters to bag a bull, any bull, with next to no regard for the quality (that is, antler size) of the bulls bagged. Following decades of this warehouse philosophy, annual post-hunt counts conducted by the Colorado Division of Wildlife began showing severely unbalanced elk herds—too few mature bulls in relation to immature bulls and cows, and too few calves per cow; the second problem being an outgrowth of the first, in that immature bulls are inefficient breeders. Things had gotten to a place where the overwhelming majority of bulls being killed were spikes (yearlings), earning Colorado a well-deserved reputation as a quantity-over-quality elk state.

Finally, a few years ago, came a fix. Following years of study and public debate, the Division imposed a moratorium on the killing of immature bulls in most game management units during most hunting seasons, since expanded to include virtually all areas and all seasons. Under this revised system, elk hunters can take only branch-antlered bulls, their three- or four-point racks being an indication that the animals have attained at least 2½ years of age. And, excepting a few heavily overhunted areas, has it ever worked! By protecting younger bulls, both herd composition and hunter satisfaction have been enhanced.

More recently—as elk numbers continue to grow, even in the face of shrinking wildlife habitat—cow permits, popular among local meat hunters, are being made more widely available. This not only takes a bit of pressure off the bulls, but helps to improve the bull-cow—and thus, cow-calf—ratio. Such necessary thinning of disproportionate female numbers is far more likely to enhance than to harm the fitness of the overall population. Moreover, reducing total elk numbers by allowing a more liberal kill will help to reduce overgrazing of limited winter wildlife range and resultant elk starvation, as well as cutting down on human-elk conflicts such as vehicle collisions and agricultural damage.

And so it is, no matter our feelings about hunting and hunters, if we want elk and other wildlife among us (and who but the emotionally dead would not?), and if we want wildlife populations to be balanced and healthy, hunting is the most effective and humane tool at our disposal.

Here in Colorado, as in many elsewheres throughout North America, thanks to carefully regulated hunting and a long chain of benevolent winters, wapiti are more numerous and the herd dynamics more balanced than at any previous time since white folk arrived and started killing elk and keeping records. In general, at least.

Exceptions must be noted: In some too-heavily hunted areas, mature bulls remain scarce and herd compositions remain out of balance. The obvious answer is to limit the number of elk hunters in these strained areas while adjusting legal limits on size and sex as necessary to nurse the herds back to health. Any hunters, or hunters' groups, who are piggish enough to squeal about such essential temporary restrictions stand as a glaring part of the problem; to hell with them and the rubber-spined bureaucrats who bow to such selfish and short-sighted demands.

But overall, at least with elk, at least here in Colorado, scientific wildlife management, using hunting as its knife, is doing more to help than to hinder natural selection in its ceaseless quest to hone the ideal beast. Hunters and nonhunters alike, squeaky wheels excepted all around, seem to trust the managers to do the right things for the long run, even if some regulations decrease some hunting opportunities in some areas in the short run, and even when mistakes are made, which of necessity in our complex, dynamic world, they often are.

While I'm among a likely minority of hunters who would enthusiastically endorse the return of as many large predators to as many public landscapes as feasible, and would gladly tithe a portion of my own hunting opportunities (and the resulting beloved wild meat) in order to share the prey with—and to receive the blessings of seeing and hearing—wolves and grizzly bears ... it will never happen. Human overpopulation, culturally inculcated greed and our ceaseless and escalating reduction of wildlands to subdivisions, clear-cuts, commercial wastelands, European-style fenced feudal playgrounds and redundant shopping malls render widespread restoration of large predators a practical impossibility. Therefore, and like it or not, we *must* rely on hunting to keep America's wildlife populations wild and strong. Fortunately, it's an efficient and flexible tool.

For another instance: The same year antler-point minimums were imposed on elk in Colorado, similar restrictions were applied to mule deer. But here the experiment backfired. Within a couple of years, those of us who were watching began noticing negative results. Many hunters who traditionally had taken the first legal buck they saw, now were being forced by law to hold out for a mature animal. Since mule deer live in more open country than elk, they're more visible and easier to kill at long distances with scope-sighted rifles, providing especially inviting targets for trophy poachers and lazy cruise-around road shooters. Consequently, big bucks began to disappear.

Belatedly recognizing the problem they'd inadvertently helped to create, the Division acted courageously to reverse the trend by removing deer antler-point restrictions in all but a handful of hunting units and limiting the buck hunt to the first three days of each of the three annual rifle seasons. For the remainder of each season, rifle hunters can take only antlerless deer, and only then if they've applied for and received a special limited-draw license.

This action addresses two obvious needs: It relieves hunting pressure on big bucks in particular, and on all bucks in general, thus allowing more males to mature; and it encourages the taking of does as a means of controlling a booming deer population before it crashes (perhaps smack into your family car some dark night).

Worthy of note is that this strategy is costing the self-supporting Colorado Division of Wildlife a bundle in deer license revenues for each year it remains in effect; not too many hunters are able or willing to pay $153.25 (nonresident), and soon to double, to hunt buck deer for just three days. This willingness on the part of the Division to forego needed income in order to do what it deems necessary for the health and balance of the deer population belies the frequent, and in some ways valid, antihunter charge that state wildlife agencies operate "game ranches" designed to maximize license sales and revenues.

While not all states are so progressive as Colorado, some are more so, and overall, scientific wildlife management works. Among its nemeses are human overpopulation (and the resulting over-hunting of some areas and species), thoughtless land development (which virtually all land "development" is), self-serving special-interest "wise use" (profit-motivated) politics, game ranching and other private commercialization of public wildlife, and an overly emotional, blithely uninformed antihunting lobby.

Which brings us back around to the topical question: Is the human hunter an "unnatural," unnaturally selective and (therefore) genetically harmful predator of cervids?

While in recent history we most certainly have been, observable, verifiable facts proclaim that in the here and now, the answer is an equivocal "no."

To begin, hunters might ask in rebuttal: Just what *is* a "natural" predator? Granting that humans evolved, quite naturally, as hunter-gatherers—what is it that makes us, and only us, "unnatural" predators today?

It's frequently said that nonhuman predators serve natural selection by eliminating old, young, sick and otherwise marginal individuals from prey populations. Certainly, this is dead true on average. Yet, it is not to say that no bear, wolf, lion or coyote ever kills a "trophy" deer or elk. What predators are selecting for is not physical condition per se, but ease of catching and overpowering a mobile meal. Occasionally if not frequently, prime male cervids, due to circumstance, become that easy meal. Here's a triad of examples to chew on:

• Biologists working in Yellowstone Park report that it's fairly common for grizzly bears to ambush and kill mature bull elk during the fall rut, when dominant males are made stupid by lust and fatigued by breeding.

• Some cougars, sometimes, would seem almost to specialize in hunting mature male mule deer. This is because, except for the weeks prior to and during the fall rut, big bucks tend to be loners, and it's much easier to sneak up on one bedded animal than to weasel through the interlocking radar defenses of a whole herd of does and fawns (or pre-rut bands of bachelor bucks).

• Cougars, coyotes and wolves kill mature, healthy deer and elk of both sexes in winter, as do grizzlies just out of den in early spring. In every case, the predators have learned to take advantage of deep snow to run down their dinner. Here, it's often the prey animal's *situation*, as much as its physical condition, that makes it vulnerable.

Just such a scene played itself out on the nearby Southern Ute Indian reservation one winter recently, when a cougar that couldn't have weighed much over 150 pounds (judging from its tracks in the snow) ran down and killed a prime 6x6 bull elk that looked to have weighed perhaps seven hundred live pounds—the relatively light-bodied, big-footed cat snowshoeing fast and easy across the surface, even as the heavy-bodied, sharp-hooved bull sank deep with every increasingly labored step, finally collapsing from exhaustion, helpless to fend off its circumstantial fate. Similar scenes occur far more often than most of us could know, might suspect or wish to admit.

This is good. Natural predation is absolutely necessary to maintain a balanced and intact ecology (literally, "household"). And modern, scientifically managed big game hunting—while it's no panacea and should never be allowed to totally supplant nonhuman predation—nonetheless is an indispensible piece of the incredibly complex predator-prey puzzle.

In conclusion, my message to "animal welfare" folk (of which I myself am a passionate one on a great many fronts) is this: If you're truly more interested in wildlife welfare than in moral censorship, withdraw your money and political support from ecologically ignorant, infinitely unrealistic hate groups, and endorse instead such noble efforts as the Rocky Mountain Elk Foundation, Vital Ground, the Nature Conservancy, Ducks and Trout Unlimited, or any of dozens of other *realistic* conservation groups working to benefit wildlife by saving wildlife *habitat*.

Given an abundance of healthy habitat, we'll always have an abundance of healthy (we could even venture *happy*) wildlife, with wisely managed hunting serving as a necessary augmentation to, and in many instances—thanks to ten thousand years of ecologically devastating agriculturalism—an essential stand-in for natural selection by tooth and claw. Further erode what little is left of quality wildlife habitat, wilderness and wildness, and *everyone* loses—predators both "natural" and vertical, "nonconsumptive" lovers of wildlife and, most painfully, the animals themselves.

For *once*, let's all try to be a little less rigid, a little more open-minded, a little less myopic and single-issue oriented, a little more willing to sacrifice, to work together for the common good.

Elk Ranching, Revisited

Since we cannot expect much truth from our institutions, we must expect it from our writers. Tolstoy said: "The hero of my work, in all of his naked unadorned glory, is truth." Thoreau said: "The one great rule of composition is to speak the truth." And that other troublemaker said, "Ye shall hear the truth, and the truth shall make ye free."—Edward Abbey

THE TROUBLE WITH TRUTH, of course, is that it's not always a verifiable commodity. And even when it is, it will still be scorned by those determined to cling to their own beliefs, no matter the luminous illogic. The archetypal example of this in our time, I suppose, is the tenacious rejection of biological evolution by literal-minded disciples of messianic religions. Who among us, at an airport or elsewhere, has not been approached by some hyper character hawking subliterate religious tracts pretending, among other things, to refute evolution and "prove" divine creation, all in the space of a comic book. God help us!

For serious seekers—those looking not to convert, but to comprehend—truth is not so often engraved on stone tablets as scratched in shifting sands. Consider the following, from Valerius Geist, writing in *Bugle* on the contentious topic of game ranching:

> Some thirty years ago ... I spied and read Raymond Dasmann's
> *African Game Ranching* and thought, now here somebody has

seen the light of day! I fell for it—hook, line and sinker. I studied and pondered game ranching for almost eight years, and even called a major conference ... in 1971 to examine the issue. I'm glad I did, for in editing the proceedings it hit me just how damaging an enterprise the commercialization and privatization of wildlife is. It hit me hard. Now I am ashamed to reflect that it took me all of eight years to see through the consequences, for on the surface it all looks so innocent and appealing.

What a relief to hear a scholar of Geist's stature make such a bold public confession—for I too am ashamed that I didn't immediately see through the superficial innocence and appeal of game ranching. Worse yet, I once abetted it. Twice, in fact.

In my slender (though not quite slender enough) pseudo-scientific tome *Racks: The Natural History of Antlers and the Animals That Wear Them* (1991), I devoted ten full pages to a simple-minded glorification of elk ranching. Those pages, in turn, began as an article for *Mother Earth News*, based on "research" conducted in 1988. Looking back, I should have put a lot more thought behind my words before inflicting them on a trusting public. Yet, I could hardly have predicted then that game ranching would soon metasticize to become, in the words of Canadian wildlife writer Kevin Van Tighem, "disease and genetic contamination factories."

The primary disease danger attendant to game ranching is bovine tuberculosis, though there's a growing list of others, all of them bred when too many animals are concentrated on too little land, and spread to wild populations by escaped captives, intrusion of wild elk into captive herds or even nose-touching through a fence.

So far as genetic contamination—as you may (or may not) recall, back in the chapter "What's In A Name?" we examined the realistic risks and disastrous consequences of red deer genes being sewn among North American wapiti by game-ranch mongrels. No point in repeating all of that here, except to note that in parts of the West, this poisonous process is already underway.

Nor are disease and genetics the only issues on this table. Game ranching is invested with serious moral flaws as well, beginning with the foundation act of imprisoning animals so intelligent, wild and energetic that they suffer unduly in their captivity. As Connie Poten, writing in *Northern Lights*, paraphrases Nobel-winning naturalist Konrad Lorenz: "The captive animals most to be pitied are the highly developed, clever ones with strong drives for locomotion, who in the wild roam far and wide. Anyone who has ever hunted elk can't help but feel awe for their keen intelligence and ability to cover long distances almost invisibly."

And anyone who has ever *ethically* hunted elk—the physically demanding, mentally challenging and gloriously unpredictable good old-fashioned hard way—should take deep personal umbrage at a second moral minus of elk ranching, arising directly from the muddy ethics of the first. I'm speaking of the rich-man's bottled and bonded shooting gallery, wherein "shooter bulls," many with pet names and tame enough to eat hay from your hand, are gunned down by ... who? What sort of "hunters" are these?

In his compact classic *Meditations on Hunting*, Spanish philosopher José Ortega y Gasset observes that "the hunter knows that he does not know what is going to happen, and this is one of the greatest attractions of his occupation." Indeed it is! If hunting were as easy as stepping out the door and killing something, I wouldn't touch it. Nor would any other serious hunter I know. The point being: A game ranch "hunt," with success guaranteed, is no hunt at all. To paraphrase contemporary hunting philosopher Ted Williams, there can be no "fair chase" when there *is* no chase.

Quite so. But no matter that no real hunter would ever think of killing a captive wild animal and wagging its decapitated and stuffed head around like a trophy, and no matter that the two leading hunters' record-keeping organizations—Boone & Crockett and Pope & Young—will have no truck whatsoever with store-bought racks, there remain a layer of clueless clowns who go blithely about their filthy business happily unburdened by any such high-flown ideals as fair chase, challenge, character, humility, compassion. If you do not hunt, don't confuse these cow-pasture killers with true hunters; they are in fact a pathetic minority detested by the ethical majority. And if you do hunt, let your outrage show! The way things are going now—given the current trend in the U.S. and Canada toward privatization of wildlife and wildlands, with the rich getting richer and the poor getting poorer and the great middle class losing ground to both, literally as well as metaphorically—in a very few decades North America could be just another Europe, where only the wealthy and powerful have hunting privileges, while the peasant majority are left to watch teevee and eat cold gruel.

Speaking of eating: There is no meat I would rather eat, and none I eat more of, than wild meat got with my own bloody hands as an ethical predatory omnivore. To the contrary, I go sick at the thought of swallowing "alternative livestock" flesh butchered from the bones of captive-raised wild animals. Magazines running plugs for high-priced eateries where "wild game" is served, as is the fashion these days, by promoting game ranching and glorifying elitist consumptive values, in fact are working against the long-term interests of wildlife and democracy. Same-same for those who proffer and purchase mail-order "wild" meat. As a hunter, I kill nothing I will not eat, I eat everything I kill, and when I fail or decline to kill, I eat road-kill. There is honor and humility in these acts. Contrarily, purchasing bogus "wild game" meat or body parts promotes wildlife profiteering, hubris, waste and worse.

A tertiary moral strike against game ranching is the cruelty, mental as well as physical, attendant to sawing off the velvet antlers of captive bull elk, to be sold like bloody gold on the booming Oriental "folk medicine" market.

I despise it all.

❦

Looking back to my misguided early praise of elk ranching, looking to forgive if not to excuse myself, the best I can plead is a dismal lack of prescience. The one elk ranch I visited in the course of my inept research pastured some three hundred elk on several hundred acres of prime elk habitat, notwithstanding the whole works was enclosed by an eight-foot fence. How could I have predicted then that a blight of tiny, often shadeless wildlife prisons were poised to erupt like zits on a teenage face, claiming the grandiloquent title "ranch," when "pen" or "feed lot" or even "concentration camp" is more often apt. While only three elk ranches existed in Colorado in the mid-1980s, the number of licensed "alternative livestock" operations as of 1998 had multiplied almost *fifty-fold*, to more than 140. Similar epidemic growth has infected other western states as well, with game ranching having become just another agricultural industry.

Not even just another, but far worse: An inherently cruel, often sleazy and potentially disastrous industry that profits few at great risk and cost to many, both human and other. Which is not to say there are no "good" elk ranchers, folks who truly care (in their own dualistic way) about their antlered "livestock"; there must be a few. But even they are inflicting pain on the intelligent, cursorial creatures they hold captive, at the same time threatening wildlife and wildlife-dependent recreation and employment throughout North America.

The initial hopes I embraced for elk ranching—the "innocent and appealing" prospects that prompted me to overlook miles of fence and canned hunts and the unanesthetized amputation of sensitive living antler (the way it was done at the ranch I visited, at that time)—these primary hopes were but two. First, considering the horrific damage inflicted on western rangelands across the past century and more by livestock, it struck me as a huge improvement to replace cows and sheep with wapiti and other wildlife, at least here and there, where climate and habitat were amenable. Rest the land, return it to a more natural state. Second, I dared to hope that if the Asian market for voodoo penis-starch derived from velvet elk antler could be glutted with legal antler, it would damage if not destroy the felonious "horn trade," wherein cowardly criminals slaughter countless prime bull wapiti, taking only their antlers.

Alas, neither of these sky-pie prophecies has proven out. In the first case, rather than resting and restoring cow-burnt, sheep-shocked rangelands to the benefit of wildlife, elk ranching, with its cumulative hundreds of miles of high fence strung across the West, utterly deprives wildlife of traditional private-land habitat, often blocking migration routes as well. As for the horn trade— rather than quenching the demand, the greatly enhanced supply of legal antler has only served to add fuel to the commercial fire, in no way slowing antler poaching and likely the opposite. So long as pride, lust, culturally sanctioned magic elixirs and bald-faced greed are with us—and when can we expect any one of these to disappear?—so will thrive the immoral, inhumane and ultimately senseless illegal trade in wild animals and their parts.

Condemning Asians for the animal abuses required to feed such perverted tastes as elk antler, rhino horn (considered an even more powerful male starch than elk antler, but equally unproven), bear gall, tiger bone, live-boiled dogs and more, is hardly racism. Rather, such criticism is a morally mandated indictment of culturally entrenched cruelty. Consider this description of a 1906 Chinese "elk ranching" operation in Manchuria, as recorded by Russian explorer V. K. Arseniev in *Dersu the Trapper*:

Near the fence was a cabin with a door, surrounded by a high palisade. It was here that the Chinese hunters performed their operation of sawing off the velvety horns of young living wapiti. Behind the hut were some cages like stalls, where the Chinese kept their deer until the antlers reached the best condition. On the right was a shed, standing on piles, in which were stored wapiti hides, dried horns, and about 350 lb. of tendons drawn from their hind-legs. Boiled horns and dried wapiti tails hung in rows from the ridgepole close under the roof. ...

"All round soon all game end," commented [Arseniev's native guide] Dersu. "Me think ten years, no more wapiti, no more sable, no more squirrel, all gone."

It was impossible to disagree with him. In their own country the Chinese have long since exterminated the game, almost every living thing.

In order for humanity and nature to survive and prosper, people, whether individuals or cultures (the latter being nothing more than assemblages of the former), *must* be held accountable for their destructive actions. To give in to the platform of political correctness—a dogma of censorship that says no culture should ever criticize another culture—is to relinquish all moral accountability. To criticize the bad is our duty to the good, eh Edward?

While we may never be able to stop wildlife criminals, or to have any great impact on how other cultures view and treat animals, we can and should at least stop condoning the legal trade in living antler here in North America—a trade that endorses and promotes animal cruelty, cultural ignorance and personal greed. Valerius Geist laid it out unflinchingly when he challenged the Canadian environmental minister: "Do we endorse bestial cruelty to elk on Canadian game ranches in order to fatten the profits of whorehouses in Seoul, Hong Kong, Bangkok and Tokyo?"

Youbetcha Canada endorses it, particularly so Alberta, which stands redneck-to-redneck with Texas as the most blatantly unconscionable pair of wildlife profiteers in all of North America.

Which is not to say that game ranching is wholly a "redneck" (i.e., churlish, lowbrow and rural) enterprise. In Canada as well as here in the States, among the movers and shakers of wildlife privateering are well-polished academics, bureaucrats, businessmen and, of course, politicians.

Among the most powerful indictments of game ranching I've yet seen is a document prepared by the Utah Division of Wildlife Resources (DOWR) in 1996, titled "Alternative Livestock (Elk Farming): Position of the Division of Wildlife Resources." From that paper, by way of introduction, this:

> In February of 1995, the Wildlife Board considered a variance to the Collection, Importation and Transportation Proclamation from a prospective Utah elk farmer to allow private individuals to possess, raise and breed live big game animals for commercial purposes. The Wildlife Board denied the variance due to the risks to wildlife populations associated with private game farms. The risks identified were: (1) disease, (2) genetic integrity, (3) feral populations and (4) commercialization and privatization of wildlife.

Following denial of the requested variance, would-be Utah elk ranchers circumvented the Wildlife Board by lobbying state legislators to enact an end-run bill legalizing elk "farming" (a more degrading term even than "ranching"). And while they were about it, the petitioners also lobbied to grant game-"farm" oversight to the Utah Department of Agriculture—in effect, firing the watch dog (DOWR) and putting Colonel Sanders in charge of the henhouse.

In response to the lobbying, a legislative committee meeting was called, wherein "progress" got its grease in the form of a draft bill authorizing "alternative livestock farming." In response, the DOWR took the admirable action of documenting "some of the problems other states associate with elk farming." With one exception, the comments of the nine states and one Canadian province surveyed were overwhelmingly negative. That exception was Nevada, who reported having "not had any problems as a result of big game farms. However, Nevada has only one big game farm in the entire state and it is a reindeer farm." From the others, some telling out-takes:

Arizona: "The Arizona Game and Fish Department reports that elk farming is legal in Arizona but the agency would not allow it if they had to do it all over again. Arizona reported the loss of huge blocks of land to fencing and some disease problems."

Colorado: "John Seidel, of the Colorado Division of Wildlife, reported that the Division used to regulate big game farming until the [Colorado Elk and Game Breeders Association] petitioned the Department of Agriculture to assume authority ... because too many citations were issued to elk farms for violations. Colorado experienced numerous poaching incidents with elk calves from the wild and theft of whole herds of wild elk captured in private farms. ... [S]ome of the larger 'elk-shooting ranches' have been investigated and charged with capturing wild [elk and deer] within the shooting preserve fences. ... [T]here have been documented problems with disease (TB), escaped hybrids and exotics, intrusion of rutting wild elk into game farms, massive recapture efforts for escapees and intruders, and loss of huge tracts of land fenced for shooting preserves/ranches. Based on their experiences, the Colorado Division of Wildlife wishes they did not have big game farms in Colorado."

Idaho: "Idaho Fish and Game once regulated elk farming in their state, but lost jurisdiction of elk farming to the Department of Agriculture as a result of pressure from elk farmers. ... Idaho has had problems with escapes and several law enforcement cases have been filed against suspects who have taken calves out of the wild for elk farming purposes."

Montana: "The state has tried to tighten regulations related to game farming, resulting in a series of lawsuits against the state from elk ranchers. ... [T]he tightening ... was in response to the discovery of TB in wildlife (elk, deer and coyotes) surrounding a TB-infected game farm. TB has been found on several game farms in Montana. Also, they have had problems with wildlife entering game farms as well as game farm animals escaping the farms. Finally ... [Montana game ranchers] allow hunters to come into enclosures to kill trophy game farm animals, raising the issues of fair chase and hunting ethics."

New Mexico: "New Mexico has problems with game farming and a moratorium on elk and game farming has been imposed by the state at the request of its citizens. Problems identified in the moratorium were: escaped game farm animals, theft of native elk herds and disease."

Oregon: "Elk farms are no longer permitted due to 'current and imminent threats to Oregon's native deer and elk herds and social and economic values.' Oregon has documented numerous game farm animals that have escaped from private game farms. ... Key [concerns expressed at public meetings leading to the ban] included disease and parasites, escape and interbreeding of domestic animals with native wildlife, illegal kills for meat and theft of public wildlife."

Washington: "Washington allows game farming, but it is strictly regulated to safeguard wildlife. Washington opposed the law when first proposed for the following reasons: introduction of disease and parasites, hybridization of wildlife species, habitat loss, health risks to humans, wildlife and livestock, and state responsibility to recover or destroy escaped elk. Game farming is not cost effective due to the restrictions needed to prevent these problems."

Wyoming: "Wyoming was sued by several game breeders associations for not allowing elk farming. The game breeders lost their suit in the U.S. Court of Appeals, Tenth Circuit. The court maintained that the state had authority to regulate commerce and protect wildlife. Wyoming has had problems with big game farming originating in surrounding states. Wyoming has documented the harvest of red deer and their hybrids during elk hunts on the Snowy Mountain range that borders Colorado. Wyoming speculates that the red deer were escapees from Colorado game farms."

Alberta, Canada: "To date [1996], Alberta has spent $10,000,000 and destroyed 2,000 elk in an unsuccessful attempt to control the spread of tuberculosis."

Other: "The [Utah] Division also contacted a Special Agent with the U.S. Fish & Wildlife Service who conducted a covert investigation in Colorado to gather intelligence on elk farming and detect poaching activity of wild elk. Although poaching was not detected, the agent described his experience with pyramid schemes in elk sales, lack of a meat market, falsification of veterinarian records for farmed elk, escapes and intrusions between wild and captive elk, inadequate inspections by brand inspectors, transportation of TB-infected elk and the temperament of the elk themselves."

Disease and Parasites: "The loss of whole wildlife herds is a heavy price for Utah to pay, should an elk farm transmit a disease or parasite to wildlife populations."

Commercialization and Privatization: "The privatization and commercialization of elk, a native big game species, compromises the tradition of wildlife resources as a public trust and jeopardizes public support for wildlife programs. The development of a commercial market for 'elk and elk products' is a concern for law enforcement and a new threat to our wildlife resources."

Habitat Loss: "Elk farmers erect high fences around their operations, sometimes cutting off wild big game migration routes and limiting movement on adjacent public and private lands. Also the private land that wildlife currently uses will be lost when these fences are constructed."

Poaching of Wild Elk: "Numerous poaching incidents for calves and trapping of elk herds for private elk farms and shooting farms have been documented. Unscrupulous elk farmers may be tempted to capture wild elk rather than pay the $8,000 to $30,000 for domestic stock. There is an established black market trade for velvet antlers, meat and trophy heads, leading to serious poaching problems on wild, free-ranging elk herds."

Hunting Farms: "Although the hunting of farmed elk is not authorized in this legislation, hunting of trophy elk is an obvious extension of this business. The hunting of captured animals will be controversial at the very least. Neither the Division nor sport hunting needs this negative publicity. Other states reported that once elk farming legislation was passed, legislation to relax elk farming regulations for hunting followed within a few years."

Animal Cruelty: "The annual blood shed during velvet antler cutting has been viewed as cruel."

Economics: "The Division has concerns whether the possible financial gain of a handful of individuals is worth the potential risks that are presented to the people of the state of Utah. The Division is also concerned about the cost that will be incurred by the state for lost or escaped elk, depredation damage to alternative livestock operations and enforcement efforts in poaching cases. Sources from other states say the antler trade has been very volatile. The main source of income for most elk operations has been the sale of breeding stock. Once breeding stock is distributed, the industry will have to find other markets to support itself. Experts in the elk industry are trying to promote the marketing of elk meat, but there is little profit at this time in the sale of elk venison. Marginal trophy bulls are sold to hunting ranches."

🍃

Again and again—disease, genetic contamination, criminal activity, cruelty, amorality. Surely, in the face of such damning evidence, no honorable, intelligent, God-fearing politicians—women and men elected and trusted to protect the welfare of the voiceless majority, as well as their states' natural resources—surely no self-respecting political body would codify such an ecologically reckless, ethically empty and economically unsound industry as game "farming."

Surely not. Yet, in the 1997 legislative session Utah *did* legalize elk "farming." Moreover, they went the requested full nine yards to hand oversight of the new "farms" to the good old boys at Agriculture.

Which brings to mind yet another Val Geist anecdote. In the course of recent Canadian election campaigns, foes of game ranching managed to extract written promises from Ralph Klein (running for Alberta Premier) and Jean Chretien (candidate for Canadian Prime Minister) to hold public hearings on game ranching if elected. "Guess what happened once they got into office?" asks a frustrated Geist. "Their agricultural bureaucracies swept that one under the carpet in a hurry! Such political dealings leave us to wonder—are senior bureaucrats running the country, instead of those we elect?"

🍃

Such a world we've made, for nonhuman others as well as ourselves. It is my conviction—my truth, backed by science, history and current events—that our Big Wrong Turn as a species, the prolonged moment comprising our pratfall from lives of relative ease, grace and dignity in an earthly, earthy garden of Eden, came with our reduction of wild sheep, goats, aurochs and other traditional prey species to "livestock." Which is to say: The biblical Fall stands as a mythopoetical account of humanity's plummeting transition from hunting and gathering to pastoralism and, hot on its heels, agriculturalism, industrialism and a slave-making, nature-killing "global economy."

Why, and how, was hunting and gathering better?

For some two million years prior to our shotgun adoption of a pastoral-agricultural lifestyle, the flesh of large wild beasts provided essential nourishment—spiritual and cultural as well as physical—for our formative humanity. Further, the organized hunting of these large, intelligent, often-dangerous wild mammals—concurrent with the gathering and preparation of edible, medicinal and psychotropic plants—necessitated and facilitated our development of true language. These same activities—practiced, refined and culturally embodied through thousands of generations—sparked our boundless passion for naming and categorizing nature, which, in turn, facilitated metaphorical thinking, the very soul of human intelligence.

In sum, hunting and gathering were the tandem engines of our "becoming human." For millennia beyond count it was so, the Sacred Game supplying us with a worldview and lifestyle at once rich, meaningful, satisfying and sustainable—*not*, as that urbane old fop Thomas Hobbes succeeded in duping generations into believing, "nasty, brutish and short." To the contrary, anthropological studies have established that hunters and gatherers—even the final few modern survivors herded by encroaching "progress" into marginal foraging habitats—work only a few days a week and view that work as pleasure, enjoying rich social, spiritual and creative lives.

So it went in the Garden of Eden, for more than 99 percent of humanity's tenuous tenure on this good green Earth. And so it could have continued for a heavenly eternity. Then, in the "holy lands," came the Fall. In an eye-blink of time, beginning some ten thousand years ago with the domestication of former prey species and their habitats and hunters, the Sacred Game was disenfranchised, desanctified, transmogrified to meaningless "product" and a hellbound cycle of production and consumption. Game ranching is a bold extension of this losing philosophy. And through it, by it, North America's wildlife heritage, past and future, is being sold ... down the river.

Daggers in the Heart

EACH AND EVERY YEAR, even as official counts tally more elk than ever before, my local Colorado mountains seem a little less crowded with wildlife, a lot more crowded with people. Insidiously, elk and other large shy animals, long my nearest and dearest neighbors, are being pushed away. And I have to tell you, it hurts—like being forced to watch, hands tied, while someone you love is tortured slowly to death.

Rust never sleeps. Corrosive change is everywhere at work. And when applied to natural dreamscapes, change is just another word for loss. Cancerous subdivision. Excoriating logging (especially devastating locally and lately on small tracts of private land, thanks in no small part to a predatory state forest service). Rampant roading ("A road is a dagger placed in the heart of wildness," said Justice William O. Douglas, and was he ever right). Green-eyed land whores and big yellow bulldozers copulating on every hillside.

Each year, millions of new "housing units" (a housing unit is not a home) are thrown up in these Untied States, and every last one of them—city, suburb and countryside alike—robbed wildlife of *their* homes. More and more, I'm coming to recognize that the heroes among us are not "instant rednecks" like me, who flee to the country, buy an acre of land, a pickup truck, a chainsaw and two big dogs—but the courageous multitudes who stick with the cities and strive to make them better, if only by becoming a little more tolerant, a little more polite, a little less wasteful and demanding.

But here I am, and here I stay. And from my boonies point of view, what's happening here (and there and everywhere as yet unspoiled) is an unmitigated mess. Urban refugees by the thousands annually join the spasmodic hegira from a hundred megalopolitan nightmares of congestion, concrete and crime, proclaiming their desire to "get closer to nature," and then—here's the rub, here's my specific complaint against many otherwise fine folk— immediately set about pushing nature away; helping to displace and destroy the very values they pretend to have come here for: the forest, the wildlife, the tranquillity.

Instances: By further subdividing their hobby ranchettes, clueless immigrants—with panting encouragement from the slavering dogs of "real estate"—rob elk and other wildings of critical highways, homes and habitat. By erecting needless fences, they fence nature out; and worse, in the case of "game ranchers," they fence wildlife in, reducing lordly wapiti to livestock with antlers, to pricey steaks in ostentatious restaurants catering to the bored and boring rich, to oriental aphrodisiacs which, as Val Geist points out, raise nothing but profits. By ignoring the commonsensical and widely advertised warning that garbage kills bears, they kill bears. By demanding of management agencies the immediate removal, dead or drugged, of virtually every wild animal that puts foot on their property, they reveal their urban-bred fears of nature. By letting their universally "harmless" dogs run unrestrained, they harass and kill wildlife by canine proxy. By complaining loud and long when any portion of any one of their bicycle or ski or snowmobile or hiking trails is closed, if only seasonally and temporarily to protect winter-stressed wildlife and spring-soaked terrain, they exemplify the grossly arrogant anthropocentric worldview that gives the terms "civilization" and "humanity" and "newcomers" and "yuppies" their increasingly bad reputations.

And all of it, at best, demonstrating an astounding ignorance of, and disinterest in, wildlife and wildlands. There are exceptions, of course—I know of a couple—and I applaud them as heroes. Nor are newcomers the only problem.

A surprising number of lifelong rural natives—owning more land, wielding more local power and generationally habituated to getting their way—are far worse; the growing "land-owner rights" movement (the current flag-waving reincarnation of the Reagan-Watt sagebrush rebellion and a co-conspirator to the profiteering "wise use" charade), which proclaims that "a man" has the right to do with "his" land as he damn well pleases and to hell with the ecology, the environment, posterity and the neighbors—this porcine "me first, me only" economic egocentrism is among the most destructive mindsets feeding on the flesh of the American West today.

Thing is—and this is no mere metaphor—we're all in the same increasingly overcrowded life raft, and if enough individuals poke even pinholes in their little corners of the boat, we're all going down together. Look around: The water is rising, the gunwales dipping beneath the waves; we're sinking already. In today's world, we can no longer disassociate individual actions and responsibilities from the commonweal, especially those actions and so-called "rights" that affect the whole. The problem, simply put, is *people*, newbie and native alike, doing all we can, fast as we can, to domesticate and masticate and defecate on what little remains of nature and small-town life: working overtime, via local chambers of commerce, to import industry and cacophony, to put an end to peace and quiet and space and beauty. This relentless "progress" is damned hard on wild hairy beasts like the wapiti and me. In fact, it breaks my bloody heart.

But what to do ... *what to do?*

Here in elk country, one thing we all can do, residents and visitors alike, is to become more informed, more open-minded and more generous regarding wildlife and wildland needs and issues, and live accordingly. Is this too much to ask?

Thing is, herbivorous mammals such as deer and elk have specific needs within the Big Four basics of forage, water, thermal and hiding cover and room to roam. As the seasons change, wildlife needs, and the habitats necessary to satisfy those needs, change as well. Winter, of course, is the hardest of times for most wild things, with different species having evolved different ways of coping, some far more effective than others. Many birds ("snow birds" included) fly the coop to warmer climes each winter. Bears and bats hibernate. But deer and elk have no such easy outs. They must adapt and cope by moving, within local bounds, to winter-friendly retreats that offer a livable combination of the essentials. Wintering wapiti and deer seek out open, tree-trimmed land; broad, lightly forested valleys and low brushy hillsides with sunny south and west exposures, where snow accumulates least and melts fastest.

Too bad for wildlife that these same sheltered, low-lying areas are "prime real estate" for humans, are largely in private ownership and are increasingly being developed. Where wapiti recently grazed and lazed on brushy foothills and expansive ranch pastures, now stand ostentatious trophy homes and tacky, crowded subdivisions, natural gas fields and industrial parks and shopping malls and high-fenced elk "ranches" and golf courses and camper parks and there ain't no end in sight.

And too, throughout elk country, huge blocks of critical winter elk habitat lie within the bounds of Indian reservations—separate nations in effect, largely beyond the management influence of state or federal agencies. Understandably, after centuries of persecution, Indians are fiercely resistant to further white interference in tribal affairs; sadly, these same nations often lack the expertise, money and vision to properly husband "their" wild-life—which, in fact, is non-Indian wildlife as well, insofar as elk and deer seasonally drift on and off the reservations. In one worst-case scenario, in Utah, Ute Indians have been trapping wild elk and selling them to private game ranches.

On the plus side, most western Indian lands remain largely un-developed, in stark contrast to the white commercial Babylons surrounding and feeding on them. And a few tribes, notably in-cluding Arizona's San Carlos and White Mountain Apaches, are proving to be admirable stewards of the wildlife that shares their lands and histories.

But across the big board, in a tragic twist of irony, many if not most modern Indians, reeling from centuries of geographical and cultural dislocation, are among those Americans least in touch with the natural world today, and consequently, no friends to wildlife. All the silly insipid New Age rage for Indian nature mysticism notwithstanding, these days, most western Indians are, in effect, cowboys. No longer able to fight their old enemies, they've joined them.

Thus, with privately owned land, red and white alike, increas-ingly denied to wildlife, it's critically important that winter wild-life habitat on public lands be wisely managed and aggressively protected, even and especially when this ruffles the feathers of a loud-mouthed minority of morons.

Of absolute necessity, to minimize harassment of winter-stressed wildlife on national forests, BLM (Bureau of Livestock Mismanagement) and state lands, motorized access—4x4s, ATVs, snowmobiles—*must be* restricted in both time and place. And on a select few delicate wildlife wintering and birthing grounds, *all* human access, muscle- as well as motor-powered, must be seasonally halted. Since most such closures run from mid-winter through the spring mud season, when human use is lowest anyhow, what's the big deal?

Incredibly, to some, newcomers and natives alike, it *is* a big deal. Here in the West, we've long since grown to expect the motorheads to rant about their "right" to tear up the landscape and harass wildlife and litter and pollute (the silence as well as the air and water), growling and screaming and whining as annoyingly and destructively as their toys. And pushing the motorized recreation crowd from behind is an oily-rich, rabble-rousing industry lobby.

Brain-damaged motorheads (all those exhaust fumes inhaled!) are old news everywhere; a given. It comes as something more of a shock to see bicyclists and cross-country skiers and campers and dog-walkers attending public meetings and writing angry letters to newspapers and politicians, raising holy hell (the only hell there is) because seasonal wildlife and wildlands needs prevent them from playing any way they want, anyplace they want, any time they want to. Of this mostly young, educated, largely yuppie set, off-road bicyclists are far and away the squeakiest wheels and seemingly the least respectful of ... well, just about everything and everyone that gets in their way. (This is a blatant generalization, I know. In truth, it's just the rude 99 percent who give all the others a bad name.)

As winter melts into spring, snow turns to mud, and soil and watershed damage threats arise. Destructive erosion can result when the wheels of vehicles—fat-tired 4x4 and ATV, and skinny-tired mountain bike alike—cut deep linear ruts in muddy roads and trails (and far too often, illegally off-road and off-trail) on steep or unstable terrain. Melting snow and heavy spring rains blast these wheel ruts to raging canals washing tons of life-giving topsoil into streams and lakes, muddying the water and suffocating aquatic life.

Even in dry conditions, wheeled vehicles (bicycles included) fording shallow streams churn up sediments that wash downstream, fouling the water and disrupting the life cycles of insects

and the feeding and spawning of fish. Similarly, human traffic—
in this case foot and horse as well as bicycle and motorized—cutting across streams or paralleling lake shores, prompts unstable
banks to collapse.

To minimize such localized ecological disasters, road and trail
closures are mandatory. And here again, those affected—including
far too many of my fellow hunters, who, forgetting that real hunting means real walking, persist in wanting to drive *everywhere*—
cry like spoiled babies taken from the teat.

Putting aside for a moment the welfare of wildlife, wildlands and
watersheds, let's examine the issue of road and trail access from a
purely human perspective: the economic bottom line. Keeping all
the tens of thousands of miles of roads criss-crossing America's
public lands (more miles than the entire interstate highway system) just passable and safe, much less *comfortable* for wheeled
travel, is financially impossible, at least given past, present and
likely future budget restrictions.

The Forest Service, as the primary example here (being victim
as well as criminal), has long since built more frigging roads—almost exclusively on behalf of loggers, almost wholly subsidized
by your tax dollars and mine—and leaves more of them open,
than it can ever come close to properly maintaining. To allow un-
restricted wet-season travel would add annual millions more to
an already staggering maintenance burden. Trails present a similar, if smaller, fiscal challenge.

For a local but nationally representative example: Across the
1.8 million acres of the San Juan National Forest in southwest
Colorado slice 2,817 miles of roads, of which only 801 miles are
closed permanently to motorized access (and too often ineffec-
tively; nothing short of complete road obliteration, significant

entry obstructions and aggressive enforcement will stop the motorheads, to whom gates and signs are but passing jokes). An additional 1,082 road miles are closed seasonally, most of which would be inaccessible in any event due to deep snow. This leaves 934 miles of forest roads open (legally if not practically) the entire year.

In all, more than half the San Juan is accessible by motor most of each year, a third is open all year, while only a quarter remains roadless—though hardly inaccessible, given the 1,125 miles of trails lacing across the San Juan. To maintain all those roads—including upkeep on forty bridges, maintenance of countless culverts, purchase and operation and repair of tons of heavy equipment, plus salaries and benefits for the ten-person maintenance crew—the San Juan National Forest, entering the millennium, has an annual budget of $600,000.

Alas and of course, the selfsame individuals and business interests who don't want seasonal road or trail closures *sure* don't want *permanent* closures and also—the greedy irony!—howl like hyenas against the levying of forest user fees or additional taxes to help pay for all that they *do* want. This is the "me-first" ditch we've dug ourselves into.

Any logical (much less altruistic) way you come at it, it's to the common good that not every square mile of our public "wild" lands be shredded into pasta with roads and trails, and not every mile of road and trail that now exists be on-demand accessible.

And of greatest urgent import: *No new roads.*

Yet—incredibly, incredulously and predictably—some 20 percent of the San Juan is marked for near-future logging, *mandating* more new roads. It's happening even now: Across the 1990s, an annual average of 12.1 miles of new roads were cut into the San Juan National Forest, largely at public expense and exclusively to facilitate private for-profit logging. The FS has proclaimed that as soon as the logging is completed, the roads will

be closed and obliterated. Based on past performance, I'll believe
it when I see it. And I don't expect to see it.

❧

What can we do—individually, collectively and painlessly—to
help ease the damage our unconscionable baby-making and ego-
centric economic growth and insatiable gluttony (lumped together, we call it "progress") is wreaking on wildlife and wild
places? What can we *do*?

As a nation, as a people united, we can rise above personalities
and petty politics to install nature-friendly "public servants"—who,
for a change, will actually serve the public, rather than powerful
special interests and themselves—and unseat nature's enemies.

As individuals, should we find a sign, a locked gate or a pile of
dirt blocking vehicle access to a public road or trail, we can view
it as an invitation to extricate ourselves from the wheeled prisons
of our SUVs and stand on our own two feet and get out and
about for some sweet fresh air, some pleasant exercise and a far
more intimate look at nature than we'll ever get through a wind-
shield. Forest roads closed to wheeled travel make quiet, verdant
pathways for hiking, horseback riding and hunting.

Concerning the latter: Wildlife managers, guides and experienced hunters agree that sitting quietly or walking slowly in the
forest is far more enjoyable, ethical and *rewarding* than motoring
up and down roads looking for easy targets. Confirming this are
statistics showing a dramatic decline in hunter success in heavily
roaded areas. In the case of elk, a primary reason for this is the
wapiti's proven preference for trackless wilderness compounded
by the fact that with too many roads, the animals have nowhere
to run to, nowhere to hide, and are quickly decimated by bucket-
seat bozos with long-range rifles.

Nor do road-caused problems end there. When hunters eliminate too many mature bulls from a herd, immature bulls do the
breeding, and do it ineptly, resulting in fewer successful pregnan-
cies, delayed calf drop and higher calf mortality from both predation (late-born elk calves, deprived of the protection of "predator swamping," are more often eaten) and winterkill (born late,
calves have less time to grow and put on life-saving weight before
facing their first winter).

Here again, as so often in life, the refusal of a few to cooper-
ate penalizes many. To be sure, penalties exist for violating road
closures—including stiff fines and being forced to tow offending
vehicles out by non-mechanical means. (I like that last one a lot.)
But for the most part, land management agencies must depend
on an intelligent, cooperative and altruistic public to recognize
and support the importance to wildlife and wildlands of road
and trail closures. Yet, more and more, not only is that necessary
trust being broken in practice, but the very concept of voluntary
self-restraint is coming under political attack.

Being good neighbors to elk and other wildlife, and to the
dwindling and tortured habitat they depend on for their very survival, especially in winter, isn't all that big a deal, isn't so much
to ask of the proud citizens of America the Beautiful.

Is it?

What the
Animals Know

I'M HIKING THROUGH A wildly beautiful Colorado mountain meadow, several miles from my camp and a thousand feet below the Continental Divide, when the sky suddenly goes dark. My day adrift in nature, I fear, is about to take a bath.

Sure enough, within minutes I'm under assault by lightning, thunder, rain like a car wash and swirling fog—your standard surprise September storm here in the high San Juans. And par for my course, my high-dollar, high-tech rain suit is back in camp, in my tent, where it won't get wet. When hail like shrapnel joins the barrage I flee like some panicked animal for the iffy shelter of the nearest finger of forest.

As I enter the dripping woods, something huge, amorphous and vaguely ominous materializes just ahead, then fades into the gloom. This is dead-center the only place in Colorado that might still hide a final few ghostly grizzlies, and my pulse quickens at the possibility. Then comes a brief thudding of hooves.

I hurry over to where the mysterious animal had been bedded, and there, at the leeward base of an umbrella-limbed old-growth spruce, I find a big oval of cushy duff scraped clean of ground litter. And dry as Noah's socks. My nose confirms it: wapiti. I gratefully claim the elk's earthy ark for my own and settle in to ride out the storm.

Amazing, the wapiti's ability to locate such efficacious refuge as this, albeit the result of mere mindless instinct, I suppose, like a dog circling before it lies down; an innate inclination hard-wired into the animal's cerebral circuits through countless millennia of selective reinforcement. Or, perhaps, finding bedding sites that will remain sheltered and dry in most any weather is a learned skill in elk, passed down from cow to calf, generation to generation. Most likely, a bit of both. The elk aren't saying.

My curiosity stirred by circumstance, and with time on my hands—perhaps all night if this storm continues—I'm soon lost in the maze of an old familiar conundrum:

What do the animals know?

Certainly, animals know more than we do about comfort, navigation, survival and other such basics of "woodcraft." Witness the ptarmigan, an alpine grouse that escapes killing blizzards by dive-bombing itself into deep, powdery snow, where it finds shelter from screaming winter winds and insulation against the sub-zero cold. Arctic fox and hares do much the same. Thus did each of these humble beasts, and others, independently invent the emergency snow cave.

At lower latitudes, desert mammals know enough to conduct their business at night and along the cool, crepuscular edges of day, then wisely hole-up in shady hide-outs during the frying hours—thus defeating dehydration, heat prostration, cataracts and scorched feet, while demonstrating a basic sort of intelligence that's rare, sometimes fatally so, among human desert rats.

And animals know enough to relax and enjoy life. A couple of autumns ago, a hiking companion and I were sitting quietly in the shade of an aspen, watching a family of mallards fool around in a beaver pond a few yards to our front. Suddenly a lone cow elk came bounding out of the woods nearby and leapt explosively into the pond, sending the ducks into panicked flight and little waves sloshing onto the shore. For the next quarter-hour, we spied as the big deer splashed, submarined, blew bubbles, kicked the water and stared, mesmerized, at the waves she made.

Clearly, this was no example of the so-called "training behavior" commonly cited by biologists as the practical motivation for play in young animals. This was a quarter-ton adult. Nor did the elk's aquatic freak-out serve any apparent practical purpose, such as escaping predators (weren't any) or drowning mosquitoes (the day was bugless). It clearly was play for play's sake.

Yet, what do such behaviors as these, impressive though they are, really say about whether or not animals possess conscious intellect—the ability to experience strong emotion, to think, reason, plan and act by self-directed choice? Not much, says traditional biology, arguing that even such seemingly spontaneous behaviors as play can be chalked up to "innate tendencies" rather than conscious intent.

So, what *do* the animals know?

🍂

It's a lot to think about, and I think about it a lot. Nor am I alone in the pursuit of this beastly koan; people have been pondering the nature and extent of animal consciousness since at least the advent of recorded history, with early students including such cerebral celebrities as Aristotle the Greek and Aesop the fable.

Even so, serious, methodical consideration of animal intelligence didn't really come of its own until the thirteenth century and the revelations of the Italian Saint Thomas Aquinas. All living things, reasoned Aquinas, have "soul." Animals are more soulful than plants because they (including we) are equipped with sensory organs—eyes, nostrils, ears—through which to gather information about our surroundings. These data subsequently are computed by this mysterious essence called soul and used to act profitably upon the world. The more soulful the animal, the more sophisticated its computation of sensory data until, with humans, soul is sufficiently powerful to facilitate self-awareness, symbolic thought, language, art, science, religion, political double-speak and all the other "higher qualities" that have brought us to our present state of arrogance, overpopulation, angst, war and widespread woe.

Not such shabby logic, St. Tom's, even by today's picky scientific standards, at least if we substitute a contemporary term— say, "intellect" or "thought" or "consciousness" or (getting fancy) "cognition"—for Aquinas's mystical "soul," and doubly impressive considering this was back when the world remained flat and intellectuals debated whether the home of the soul was the heart or the brain; even the bloody liver had its champions.

Aquinas's placement of the various species on an ascending intellectual scale, like the rungs of a ladder, remained more or less in vogue until the 1600s, when *all* animals' souls were rudely repossessed by the French anthropocentrist René ("I think, therefore I am") Descartes, the so-called father of so-called modern philosophy. Echoing the religious dogma of his day, Descartes preached that animals were created expressly for human use and are, by Divine Design, devoid of soul—mere senseless automatons, flesh-and-bone machines, fur-covered robots lacking any shred of consciousness or feeling.

"There is," proclaimed Descartes in his *Discourse on Method*, no supposition "more powerful in leading feeble minds astray from the straight path of virtue, than that the soul of brutes is of the same nature with our own."

Even the screams of beasts in pain, in Descartes's hard-hearted view, were nothing more than the screeches of damaged machinery: *vox machina*. To "prove" his theory, Descartes nailed his family dog to a wall and set about dissecting the living, writhing, screaming animal in search of a physical soul ... and, I propose, forfeited his own soul in the doing.

Handy, this "Cartesian dualism" worldview, with humans the Chosen Ones of creation and all the rest of nature relegated to the senseless side of the tracks. Buy into this one, and we have moral license to use and abuse animals any old way we wish, conveniently unburdened by conscience, empathy or "humanity."

And abuse animals we did, and of course still do. Consider the assembly-line oppression of industrial animal-farming. Consider the forced containment and annual mutilation of the great wild wapiti for ego and profit. Consider every American neighborhood's many examples of criminal neglect of *Canis familiaris*, "man's best friend," kept caged in small apartments or chained in suburban backyards, gradually turning loud and psychotic and mean from neglect and frustration. And consider, *please*, the living nightmare of vivisection, that blood-splattered laboratory of Nazi Dr. Doolittle tortures inflicted on countless animals daily ("How smart," asks celebrity scientist Carl Sagan, "does a chimp have to be before killing him constitutes murder?"), most often for purely commercial or scientifically redundant ends rather than to gain vital new medical knowledge. Descartes would be pleased to know that we are *still* cutting up living dogs.

Beyond the sylvan shelter of my natural umbrella, the tempest rages on. The lightning and thunder have jumped the Divide and are moving away now, and the hail has petered out. But the wind still howls like some frenzied beast and rain pours with redoubled vigor from a ruptured firmament. And here I squat, carefree as a Caliban, playing mind games with myself.

Thankfully, all things pass, including René Descartes, whose arrogant old soul now resides in an exclusively human heaven where winged angels sing but hermit thrushes and canyon wrens do not, and no lowly deer or antelope are allowed to play. Sounds like hell to me. As it did to a whole menagerie of post-Cartesian thinkers, including one Percy Bysshe Shelley, an early nineteenth century English poet of some small renown who opined that "the monstrous sophism that beasts are pure unfeeling machines, and do not reason, scarcely requires a confutation."

Likewise, the Scottish philosopher David Hume attacked the Cartesian legacy by asserting "no truth appears to me more evident than that beasts are endow'd with thought and reason as well as men."

In his turn, the German thinker Arthur Schopenhauer added yet more fuel to the Cartesian funeral pyre with the opinion that even though they lack true language, animals nonetheless possess conscious understanding and can exert free will.

And so on, through a lengthy litany of philosophical hypotheses and opinion, far more often than not coming down on the animals' side.

But philosophy, alas, *is* mere hypothesis and opinion—albeit thoughtfully, elaborately, even eloquently voiced—and as hypothesis and opinion, it fails definitively to answer the query at hand: What do the animals *know*?

Only in the twentieth century did there finally appear a school of serious scientific investigation into animal intelligence, perhaps too serious. Its name was behaviorism, and its guru was an animal researcher painfully familiar to all veterans of Psych 101—B. F. Skinner.

Intrigued by the work of that infamous Russian dog trainer "Drooling Ivan" Pavlov, Skinner specialized in tormenting animals by crowding them into small cages, forcing them through endless mazes, surgically implanting electrodes in their brains, and worse, all in hopes of demonstrating, among other things, that for every stimulus (say, stuffing ever more rats into a small box), there follows a predictable response (ever more depression, aggression, murder, rape, incest, psychosis and other all-too-familiar urban social ills).

Behaviorism quickly came to so totally dominate the scientific study of animal intelligence that for decades researchers with conflicting ideas and data were reluctant to publish their views for fear of professional ridicule—hardly the open-minded atmosphere necessary for doing good science.

Only relatively recently has fundamentalist behaviorism finally begun to lose ground to the far kinder and gentler school of cognitive ethology. Cognition is just a five-dollar word for all that's involved in conscious thought, while ethology is the study of animal behavior, under more or less natural, as opposed to harshly clinical, conditions. In the old days, we'd have called it "nature observation."

And old it is. As early as the fifth century B.C., a Greek slave writing under the name of Aesop dabbled in cognitive ethology when he celebrated in fable a raven he'd seen dropping small stones into a narrow-necked jug half-full of water, thus incrementally raising the level of the liquid until the bird could reach it for a drink. More than two millennia later, in a treatise called *Advancement of Learning,* English historian and philosopher Sir Francis Bacon echoed Aesop when he asked rhetorically, "Who taught the raven in a drought to throw pebbles into a hollow tree, where she espied water, that the water might rise so as she could come to it?"

Recent experiments conducted by University of Vermont cognitive ethologist Bernd Heinrich validate the raven's far-flung reputation for ingenuity. After suspending a bit of food on a long string below a perch pole, Heinrich photographed one of his birds solving the problem by lifting a length of string with its beak, then anchoring the coil to the perch with a foot, over and over again, until it had literally reeled in the bait. (Crows, on the other hand, never got past grabbing the suspended morsel on the fly, only to have it jerked rudely from their beaks.)

Equally impressive, a second raven, watching the first, didn't merely ape what it saw, but immediately improved on the technique by grasping the string loosely in its beak and walking the length of the perch pole to draw it up, thus bringing home the bacon with more speed and less effort.

Similarly, cultural anthropologist Richard Nelson, in his award-winning natural history *The Island Within,* reports that ravens are said by the Koyukon Indians of interior Alaska to lead hunters to game, but only those hunters whose hearts are good. Having repeatedly witnessed and paid attention to this fascinating behavior myself, I too have come to view the raven as a hunter's helper. At least on occasion.

Like so: I'm either sitting quietly or creeping slowly through the woods—bowhunting for my winter's supply of wild meat, photographing wildlife or merely looking—when ravens, usually a pair, appear and circle low overhead, croaking grandly as if to proclaim *Look! Look!* Our relationship thus established, the birds clam up and scram. Then, sooner more often than later, the same ravens sound off again, now from a near distance and in harsher, more urgent tones, repeating a call that I've come to hear as *Elk! Elk!* (In the Koyukon language, says Nelson, it translates as *Animal! Animal!*)

Through conditioning, I've learned to perk up at such times, for once in a while—not often, but often enough to be of serious note—the birds are hazing deer or, more often, elk.

I'm no bleeding-heart, Bambi-brained nature mystic, and neither are Drs. Nelson and Heinrich, both of whom are fascinated by the special "working" relationships they've observed between ravens and large mammalian predators—in Nelson's case, those predators are men; in Heinrich's observations, wolves. Nor is anyone suggesting that ravens are attempting to establish some Voodoo New Age connection with humans.

Rather—it's perfectly obvious—the big bright birds are simply displaying practical intelligence—working for wages, as it were, in the form of offal and meat scraps left behind by the hunters they help, human and otherwise. The conscious intellect implied here—visualizing a profitable end, conceiving a strategy, recognizing and recruiting allies, communication, persistence—is rich food for thought.

But then, any staunch behaviorist will eagerly inform you that "innate behavior patterns" can provide animals with an impressively broad choice of responses to apparently unique stimuli, leaving unsophisticated observers (like me) with the false impression that thinking has happened.

Certainly, that *can* be the case. But, I wonder, does it *have* to be? Not so with the human beast; witness our complex hodgepodge of innate *and* intellectual behaviors. Why then always so in other animals? I find it easier to believe that the occasional Einstein of a raven has intellect enough to purposely join forces with hunters or conceive the simple dynamics of liquid displacement (although we all know *people* who couldn't do either), than to accept that natural selection would bother to imprint such complex, individualized and unpredictable responses in instinct.

For those seriously interested in such arcane corners of nature, there are bookfuls of scientifically documented near-human intellectual feats performed by animals of every feather, from pigeons to primates. In summarizing a few such high points, science writer James Shreeve, in *The Neandertal Enigma*, reminds us that ...

> Given a little training, chimps and gorillas can communicate by
> using symbols, teach each other sign language and, by some

accounts, even discuss their emotions and ideas of death with their trainers. We now know that even in the wild, vervet monkeys utter different alarm cries depending upon what sort of danger is imminent—perhaps the beginning of language. ... Lions hunt cooperatively, wolves share food, elephants regularly display an emotional depth more profound than, say, some modern human beings working on Wall Street.

And a lot like some modern human beings working on Wall Street, animals are not above deceiving one another for personal gain. Among the best-documented animal "liars" is the piping plover, which deftly decoys predators away from its ground nests by employing such inventive dramatics as flopping off with a faked wing injury or squeaking like a rodent from behind a screen of tall grass—the style of the pretense cleverly tailored to fit the nature of the threat, the appetites of the predator. As long ago as 1833, John James Audubon wrote of the piping plover ...

> You may see the mother, with expanded tail and wings trailing on the ground, limping and fluttering before you, as if about to expire; [but] when the bird has fairly got rid of her unwelcome visitor, and you see her start up on her legs, stretch forth her wings and fly away piping her soft note, you cannot but participate in the joy that she feels.

Similarly, I've had elk cows and mule deer does boldly attempt to decoy me away from their hidden infants when I've stumbled too close.

While James Shreeve praises the extensive predator-alarm vocabulary of vervet monkeys, even more impressive is that these fiercely territorial primates employ their "beginning of language" to deceive one another. When a home-team clan of vervets is under attack by an invading clan and the battle seems all but lost, one or more of the defenders may suddenly start screaming the universal vervet equivalent of "Leopard! Let's get *out* of here!" It's the most urgent, frightening and powerful phrase in the vervet repertoire and it invariably sends the invaders packing. No mere monkey business, this, but conscious, cunning psychological warfare.

Yet, such deceits as the vervet's and plover's are "honorable" lies told not for greedy ends but to protect home and family. More self-serving, and thus more humanlike, are the talented imitations of screeching raptors uttered by Steller's jays as they swoop in on my bird feeder, effectively clearing the crowded perch of chickadees, nuthatches, juncos and even other jays. Do "selfish" acts such as this not suggest a thoughtful, creative, one might even venture *Machiavellian* intelligence?

Deceit aside, a singularly impressive example of what appears to be high-order animal intellect was related to me by nationally respected black bear biologist Tom Beck. Your standard live-trap for bears consists of a length of large-diameter steel culvert pipe with one end capped shut and the other equipped with a heavy guillotine door that slides up between parallel tracks and is held open with a sturdy metal pin. When a bear enters the big barrel and tugs the baited trigger mechanism, the pin is pulled, allowing the door to slam shut and trap the bear within.

Says Beck: "I've watched bears who've never seen a culvert trap walk up to one, check it out from various angles, then stand up, grab the door and with a powerful twisting motion wrench it sideways, bending and binding it in the open position ... then they step inside, take the bait and stroll away."

This same widely experienced field biologist also reports seeing bears toss rocks or sticks onto the triggers of spring-activated leg snares to disarm them before going in for the goodies. "Bears," Tom Beck will tell you, "appear to be capable of reasoning, planning and spontaneous problem solving."

Seconding Beck is grizzly expert Doug Peacock, who holds that grizzly bears are smart enough to know when they're being tracked, are aware of their own footprints and sometimes take pains—such as walking in water or on rocks while avoiding snow and mud—to throw hunters and hounds off their trail, even backtracking to lie in hiding and watch (and, we may presume, chuckle at) their confused pursuers.

And one last anecdote from Tom Beck: In winter, in a shallow creek whose water had frozen solid, Tom found where a deer had pawed a substantial amount of dirt out onto the ice. Curious, the biologist checked in again the following day, only to discover that the deer had returned to lap up the muddy melt-water.

"I'm not saying that deer understand and consciously employ the principles of solar heating," Beck cautions, "but I do know that a deer intentionally pawed dirt onto ice and the same deer returned later to the same spot to drink from the little pool of water melted by the heat absorbed by the dark-colored dirt."

Even so—all these feats of apparent animal intelligence and plenty more notwithstanding—it remains that without a complex spoken language with which to symbolize, share and refine whatever knowledge they possess, animals are doomed (or perhaps blessed) never to enjoy (or perhaps endure) the abstract mental abilities that define the human mind. (Just try thinking without words.) Some theorists even posit that language *is* consciousness.

What do the animals know?

Wild animals, above all, know The Secret of Life, as proven by their ability to exist in perpetual balance (though not necessarily in mutual harmony) with their fellow creatures and with the environment that sustains us all. It's a basic, absolutely essential quality of intelligence that *Homo saps* long shared, but began to lose ten millennia ago when we took our first big bite from the forbidden fruit of superfluous knowledge, leading straight-away to the Big Fall from the infinitely sustainable grace of a natural existence, from the nurturing womblike warmth of clan-based hunting and gathering cultures—down, down—into a filthy dungeon of endless agricultural drudgery, cancerous population growth, cruel class structure, environmental genocide and all the other ugly produce of modern man's (and woman's) mindless mania for so-called progress.

But ask now the beasts, and they shall teach thee; and the fowls of the air and they shall tell thee. Or speak to the earth, and it shall teach thee.

Fat chance, Job.

As suddenly as it appeared, the wind now dies. The rain fizzles to a drizzle, and stops. And thanks to the practical intellect of the cud-chewing ungulate who led me to this sheltered nest I'm squatting in, I've ridden out the most horrendous storm of the summer without rain gear and sitting pretty—pretty dry, pretty warm, pretty comfortable, pretty grateful.

Intelligence, I reckon, is what works best to satisfy a species' needs *within the niche in which it finds itself.* I mean—what use would an elk have for a Ph.D. in nuclear physics? For that matter, what good have such reckless intellectual gymnastics done *us*?

It has been proposed that even if we could find a way to talk with the animals, what they had to say would be Greek to us, so different is their perception and "processing" of the world from our own. "All the thoughts of a turtle are turtle," surmised good old Ralph Waldo. Clearly this is so—so, why then do we persist in trying to quantify and qualify animal intelligence on the human model?

So many questions, so few answers.

I stand and stretch and weave amongst the dark dripping trees, back out into the big montane meadow I'd been waltzing through when my halcyon hike was so rudely interrupted some hours ago. In the nonce, night has slammed down hard and black as obsidian, erasing all landmarks and shifting my mood from philosophical to paranoid: Where the hell *am* I, and which way back to camp?

From out in the inky void rises an eerie fluted wail, tailing off into a staccato series of coughing chuckles. My reluctant antlered innkeeper, no doubt, enjoying the last laugh. My navigational worries notwithstanding, I have to smile. The wapiti's bugle, like the tumbling crescendo of a canyon wren, is a language imbued with more mystery, magic, passion and *sustainable* intellect than we space-walking humans are ever likely even to comprehend, much less equal.

That beast out there is already home, while I have yet to find my way.

Afterword

ALTHOUGH HE DID A bit of wild-meat poaching in his earlier, hungrier years, my old friend Edward Abbey never was much of a hunter, especially toward the end—he was too busy writing wildly popular novels and life-changing essays and exploring and defending western America's shrinking wilderness. Yet Ed was supportive of his many ethical-hunter friends and a voracious lover of the venison and elk jerky we gave him.

Today, some wrong-headed hunters put Abbey in the enemy camp because of his staunch environmentalism and outspoken criticism of some of the more egregious aspects of hunting. In truth, Abbey worked harder and accomplished more to assure a future for public-lands wildlife, and thus, a future for democratic (as opposed to rich-man's private-preserve) hunting, than any so-called "hunter's rights" group past or present. Let me explain.

I first met Ed Abbey in the early 1980s in his hometown of Tucson, where I'd gone to interview him for a magazine story. When I brashly inquired if he were an atheist, he sternly replied (in that trademark booming bass voice), "I am an *earthiest* ... I stand *for* what I stand *on*."

Earthiesm, as I've since come to understand and embrace it, is nothing more or less than contemporary animism. And an animist, of course, is nothing more or less than a heathen, that primitive, savage, uncivilized beastly human form described by Ambrose Bierce as "a benighted creature who has the folly to worship something that he can see and feel."

Bingo!

Through a long slow process of personal and philosophical maturation, in which watching, studying, helping, hunting, dreaming and, withal, *living* elk and other wildlife has played a dominant role, I too have come to think of myself as an animist, an earthiest, a heathen. You might even say that animals made me human. Like Cactus Ed, I believe the most logical and rewarding course is to live just one life at a time, and as much of it as possible out and about in the earthly heaven of wild nature.

Which is to say: Any afterlife lacking bugling September elk, golden autumn aspens chattering in a clean mountain breeze, wild trout leaping for joy in clear cascading water, the lusty spring gobbling of wild turkey toms and the humbling *aliveness* that comes with the possibility of meeting a bear or lion just around the next bend in some remote unknown trail, the indescribable ecstacy of love on the rocks, the spicy flavor of a good cheap cigar, the smoky bouquet of a fine Irish single-malt—any pie-in-the-sky heaven lacking such earthly blessings would be for me a madman's hell.

When I was a boy coming up on the windswept, farmed-out and eroded red-dirt Oklahoma plains—I'm talking the late 1950s and early '60s—the only big game animals around were white-tailed deer, and even those were precious few and far away. I didn't see one in fact until I went deer hunting for the first time at age fourteen. Then, through a week of hard trying, I saw a few. I was old enough to hunt but too young to drive so my father, who worked too much and had little time and less inclination to hunt or fish, made amends by chauffeuring a school pal and me two hundred miles east to a place where clustered second-growth pines furred a bumped-up landscape and ghostly whitetails lurked. Dad hauled us and our little pile of Boy Scout camping gear as far back into the woods, via an obstacle-course logging trail, as he could coax his Ford wagon, wished us luck and turned around for home and another long day of work after the all-night drive. That week proved an epiphany and a blessing, and a week in the late November deer woods became a cherished annual ritual.

On those youthful expeditions I camped and hiked and explored and got terrifyingly lost and viewed it all as a pilgrimage—I'm dead serious about this: Those early hunting trips *were* pilgrimages; adventures of spiritual discovery and growth. The deer were ephemeral alien beings, more spirit than flesh, and the piney woods through which they ghosted were sacred groves. Gradually, hunting love would lead to nature love and nature love to a heartfelt conservation ethic—and that ethic and the love behind it to my present happy condition as a born-again animist ... an earthiest, if you will.

For that one week and that week alone, I felt fully alive and realized. One such week a year of course wasn't nearly enough, and I returned home each fall with a deep and poignant hunger brooding in my soul. (I still do, though now I pursue deer, elk, pronghorn, turkey and grouse across many weeks each year.)

And so it was that what would come to be a life-guiding affinity for the natural world, for shaggy *wild* as opposed to natty pastoral nature, was born—not as you might expect, of a richness of early experience, but rather—of deprivation. Supply and demand. I had too little wildness in my young suburban life and, my appetite whetted by those annual hunting outings, I craved a great deal more.

Following a six-year (de)tour with the Marines and various other wanderings that allowed for precious little hunting or fishing or other adventures in nature, I came to settle here in rural western Colorado, where I set about reinventing my boyhood discovery of wildness and freedom. But rather than the rolling hills of my youth, here are mountain peaks that rip the bellies of brooding clouds. Rather than second-growth piney woods, here stand vast dense forests of old-growth spruce, fir and ponderosa, illuminated in autumn by pyrotechnic clones of quaking aspen. And the beasts that lend magic to my life are no longer white-tailed deer, but big-eared muleys, bears and, most especially, wapiti.

Tragically, wide and wild wapiti habitat throughout North America is under fierce and relentless attack. And in large measure, this destruction of our shrinking wildlands, our imperiled national treasure of elk-quality wilderness—is facilitated by politicians who get themselves elected by professing to be defenders of "sportsmen's rights," while in fact fronting for rapacious molesters of the habitat upon which wildlife—and thus, hunting and fishing (and all the rest)—depend. For some of the most dismal environmental voting records in Washington, year after year, look to the so-called Congressional Sportsmen's Caucus.

Which is to say, to pointedly point out, that far, far too often, we hunters, through thoughtlessness and ignorance, are helping to kill the very things we love.

My most earnest earthiest's prayers, therefore, are that sportsmen and women (soon and for a change) will learn to vote the big picture and the long-run rather than continuing to be duped into helping elect enemies of wildlife, wildlands and ultimately of hunting's future. That we as a culture, a nation, a species (soon and for a change) will find more and better ways to bring sanity and restraint to today's insane and unrestrained population growth. (*When* will we ever find the courage and resolve to *seriously* address *that* worn-out old taboo?) That we "owners" (in fact mere ephemeral custodians) of America's forests, fields and streams will strive to effect a wiser and vastly more prudent approach to the "improvement" of our private "real estate."

Soon for all of this. Before it's too late. For everyone and everything. Forever.

"After we've lost a natural place," writes anthropologist, hunter-conservationist and award-winning natural historian Richard Nelson, "it's gone for everyone—hikers, campers, boaters, bicyclists, animal watchers, fishers, hunters and wildlife— a complete and absolutely democratic tragedy of emptiness."

You said it, Nels: gone, gone and ... gone.

Not that nobody's trying. The ethics education of its hundred-thousand-plus members, conducted through *Bugle* magazine, plus the habitat conservation, preservation and restoration work being accomplished by the Rocky Mountain Elk Foundation and a precious handful of other sportsmen's conservation groups, is of critical import and the gains are visible.

Yet, enhancing the outdoor ethics and conservation conscious-ness of *only* sportsmen is hardly enough. Unless all of humanity soon develops and sustains a significantly more charitable and familial view toward the nonhuman world—we could call such a paradigm earthiesm—this shrinking Eden, this garden of earthly paradise with which we've been so incredibly blessed by the in-scrutable mysteries of natural creation, will continue to erode and the quality of our lives erode with it, until we and our children and their children and theirs are left to wander dazed and lost through days gone gray as urban concrete, suffocating in the memory of what was here once and was meant to last forever, but now is gone. This is not some gloomy pessimist's forecast, but open-eyed observation of a process already well underway.

And among the first of our land-based freedoms lost will be hunting. Without large expanses of natural habitat in which wild animals can wander and hunters wander after them, both "hunter's rights" and "animal rights" become superfluous. What Edward Abbey was trying to tell us is that *it doesn't have to be that way.*

But only by pulling together can we who understand and care—hunters, nonhunters and antihunters alike—hope to save what little is left of truly wild nature ... of the fur-fin-and-feather bed in which our species was conceived, and which without we surely will wither and die.

Just because, a month a year, I prey on elk with primitive carnivorous passion, does that negate my knowledge and understanding of these magical creatures? Does it negate my *love* for them? Does pursuing what Paul Shepard, in deft double entendre, calls "the Sacred Game" (the *elk* is the sacred game; the elk *hunt* is the sacred game)—does being a passionate player in this most essential drama of life on Earth mandate that such a one knows and loves the wapiti less?

If so ... who loves the wapiti more?

Colorado's monthlong elk and deer archery seasons closed last week. Of those thirty legal hunting days, I hunted twenty-seven; not all day every day, sorry to say, but four hours or more, mostly evenings, for twenty-seven of the thirty given days. And all I killed was time. It's become my norm these past few years, hunting more and killing less, prompting Caroline to tag me with the nickname Elkheart. Even when, craving their meat, I do kill one of the animals in whom I invest so much time, energy and love, Caroline remains a skeptic, calling it "an anomaly."

"He's changed over the years," she'll tell you, only half joking. "These days, he doesn't want to *kill* an elk nearly so much as he wants to *be* an elk."

Well, truth be known, I'd rather be a grizzly bear.

But yes, it's fact that in our earliest years living here I was driven by hunter's insecurity and poverty-induced hunger to kill

the first legal animal that came along—spike, cow, whatever—
and I did so with clockwork consistency. Friends thought of me
as a meat hunter and a good one though there was a lot more to
it than that. These days I don't know what kind of hunter I am.
All I know is, my passions for elk and the hunt burn hotter than
ever, and my love for the two is inseparable one from the other.

Oddly enough, my growing passion for the hunt explains why
I kill less, and less often, as the years spin past: Killing, you see,
kills the hunt. The September bow season is the apogee and
apotheosis of my outdoor year and one of the greatest pleasures
I take from life. Having a precise goal beyond merely watching—
and a keenly demanding goal it is, shaking awake and bringing
back into play millions of years of evolved instinct and the joy
that accompanies doing what we are physically and mentally *intended* to do—having such a goal puts an electric edge on everything, producing a true "natural high" of sensory and spiritual
experience.

So why rush to end it all?

Why reduce a potential month of hiking and camping and exploring and getting lost (and, so far, found again) and watching
and loving and learning—why abbreviate four weeks of such un-
fettered joy to mere days, or even hours, in response to some
senseless sense of urgency? A young man fears that by going too
slow, he risks missing something. An older man knows that to go
too fast is to risk missing everything. Most assuredly, I want to
"succeed"; I want the lean, delicious, untainted meat and the
warm satisfaction of a challenge overcome. And too, yes indeed,
I want those big beautiful antlers on my wall. But, in the end,
more and more, what I want most is the hunt itself.

I'll think about all of this often through the long cold months
ahead, and it will help. While I sit in my wood-warmed cabin
whiling the winter away—feasting on road-killed venison, sipping

Irish whiskey and growing softer by the day—the elk remain *out there*, growing stronger and wilder by the day; like me, impatiently awaiting the rebirth of spring.

For the man or woman blessed and cursed with a hunter's heart, deserting the woods at season's end is like a soldier leaving a lover he (or she) won't see again for long lonely months, maybe never (so many things can happen). For me, the pain of this annual parting is real, an ulcerous fire burning deep in my guts. No wonder the ancients viewed the heart, not the head, as the seat of love and desire.

Love and longing. Aching nostalgia. The tumultuous passions of the soul. The bitter-sweet, tear-salty tang of good times relived in memory. Ironically—have you ever noticed?—the more precious the person or place or experience recalled, the more painful the memory ... exactly because it reminds us that those priceless times, relationships and, most of all, *unrealized possibilities* are gone. Forever.

Again, it was Abbey who said it best ...

In my imagination, desire and love and death lead through the wilderness of human life into the wilderness of the natural world—and continue, round and round, perhaps forever, back again to wherever it is we began.

And where we all began was with the hunt.

For those few among us in whom those ancient animal/animist instincts remain vital, little has changed. No one, biologists notwithstanding, knows or cares more about the natural histories and daily dramas of animals in the wild, no one is a more attentive student of animal spoor (the first abstract art, the first written language), no one more deeply and honestly loves wildlife and wild lands and freedom and dignity, than the hunter. The *true* hunter, that is, as opposed to the legions (lesions) of dilettantes, poseurs, gadgeteers, privateers and profiteers infesting and infecting the sporting ranks today.

I hunt elk for the selfsame reason I study them and watch them and fight to protect them—I do it all for love. For love of the great grand beasts themselves. For love of the fierce magic mountains they animate. For love of the freedom they embody and the joyful jolt of adrenaline their earthy animal essence sends surging through my being. And I kill them (when we both are good and ready) in order to bring their strength into my body, their beauty into my home, their wildness into my life. I hunt elk because I love elk. I love the Sacred Game.

I am Elkheart, after all.

Selected Bibliography

Abbey, Edward. *One Life at a Time, Please.* New York: Henry Holt & Co., 1988.

Arseniev, V. K. *Dersu the Trapper.* Malcolm Burr, trans. New York: McPherson, 1996.

Beck, Thomas. Colorado Division of Wildlife. Personal communications, 1988.

Bugle. Missoula, MT: Rocky Mountain Elk Foundation, various issues, 1986–1998.

Cornish, Vaughn. *Scenery and the Sense of Sight.* Cambridge: Cambridge University Press, 1935.

DeByle, Norbert V., and Robert P. Winokur, eds. *Aspen: Ecology and Management in the Western United States.* Fort Collins, CO: USDA Forest Service General Technical Report RM-119, no date.

Geist, Valerius. *Elk Country.* Minocqua, WI: NorthWord Press, 1991

———. "Public Elk, Private Profit: The Perils of Selling Wildlife," in *Bugle.* Missoula, MT, May–June 1998.

———. Personal communications, 1998.

Hall, E. Raymond, ed. *Mammals of North America,* 2nd edition. New York: John Wiley & Sons, 1981.

Herrero, Stephen. *Bear Attacks.* New York: Nick Lyons Books, 1985.

Murie, Olaus J. *The Elk of North America.* Jackson, WY: Teton Bookshop Publications, 1979.

Noyes, James H., et al. "Effects of Bull Age on Conception Dates and Pregnancy Rates of Cow Elk," in *Journal of Wildlife Management,* 60(3):508–517, 1996.

Ortega y Gasset, José. *Meditations on Hunting.* Howard B. Wescott, trans. Bozeman, MT: Wilderness Adventure Press, 1995.

Petersen, David. *Among the Elk.* Flagstaff, AZ: Northland Publishing, 1988.

———. *Racks: The Natural History of Antlers and the Animals That Wear Them.* Santa Barbara, CA: Capra Press, 1991.

———. Personal communications, 1946– .

Poten, Connie. "Altered States: Game Farms," in *Northern Lights.* Missoula, MT: Spring 1994, Vol. X, No. 1.

Seidel, John. Colorado Division of Wildlife. Personal communications, 1998.

Seton, Ernest Thompson. *Lives of Game Animals,* Vol. III. Garden City, NY: Doubleday, Doran & Co., 1927.

Shepard, Paul. *The Tender Carnivore and the Sacred Game.* New York: Scribners, 1973.

———. *The Others: How Animals Made Us Human.* Washington, D.C.: Island Press, 1996.

———. *Traces of an Omnivore.* Washington, D.C.: Island Press, 1996.

Shepard, Paul, ed. *The Only World We've Got: A Paul Shepard Reader.* San Francisco: Sierra Club Books, 1996.

"Status of Elk in North America: 1975–1995." RMEF Special Report Number 1. Compiled by S. Dwight Brunnell. Missoula: Rocky Mountain Elk Foundation, 1997.

Thomas, Jack Ward, and Dale E. Toweill, eds. *Elk of North America: Ecology and Management.* A Wildlife Management Institute book. Harrisburg, PA: Stackpole Books, 1982.

Utah Division of Wildlife Resources. "Alternative Livestock (Elk Farming): Position of the Division of Wildlife Resources." Salt Lake City, Nov. 18, 1996 (as published on the Internet).

Van Tighem, Kevin. "The Land Ethic: Dead Pines and Wise Use," in *The Outdoor Edge.* Canada, Nov.–Dec. 1995.

Williams, Ted. "The Elk-Ranch Boom," in *Audubon.* New York, May–June 1992.

———. Personal communications, 1998.

Wolfe, Gary J. "Population Dynamics of the Vermejo Park Elk Herd, with Special Reference to Trophy Management." Unpublished doctoral dissertation, Colorado State University, 1985.

About the Author

(so-called)

DAVID PETERSEN is a middle-aged recovering Marine Corps helicopter pilot, a reformed mailman, magazine editor and college teacher who, through it all and in spite of having the perfect credentials, has somehow avoided "going postal." So far.

David lives, within his humble means, in a tiny, self-built, aspen-warmed pine cabin in the San Juan Mountains of southwest Colorado in the company of his long-suffering wife, Caroline, and their two huge ferocious guard dogs, Otis and Angel (both of whom know the difference between uninvited human visitors and welcome wildlife neighbors, harassing the former while quietly suffering the latter). When pressed, Petersen admits to being a "de facto derivative" naturalist, a "craven" preservationist, a "half-assed" hunting ethicist/reformer/defender and, withal, "somewhat" eccentric. He is the perpetrator of nine previous books, all of which have met with generous acclaim and parsimonious sales.